Living Religions

Islam

Andrew Egan

Raintree, 100 N. LaSalle St., Suite 1200, Chicago, IL 60602

Library of Congress Cataloging-in-Publication Data:

Egan, Andrew.
 Islam / Andrew Egan.
   v. cm. -- (Living religions)
Includes bibliographical references and index.
Contents: An introduction to Islam -- The Prophet Muhammad (PBUH) -- The prophets -- Muslim leadership and authority -- Muslim beliefs -- Allah -- Thinking about Allah -- Signs and symbols -- Worship-shahadah -- Worship-salah 1 -- Worship-salah 2 -- Worship-sawm -- The mosque -- Holy books-the Koran -- Holy books-Hadiths -- Celebrating festivals -- Pilgrimage-Hajj 1 -- Pilgrimage-Hajj 2 -- Rites of passage -- Creation -- Environment -- Abuses of Allah's creation -- Human rights -- Caring for others-zakah -- Women in Islam -- Matters of life and death -- Jihad -- Evil and suffering -- The existence of Allah.
 ISBN 0-7398-6385-1 (Library Binding-Hardcover)
 1. Islam--Juvenile literature. [1. Islam.] I. Title. II. Series.
 BP161.2 .E37 2003
 297--dc21
                          2002152097

Printed and bound in China.

07 06 05 04 03
10 9 8 7 6 5 4 3 2 1

Acknowledgments
The author would like to thank Imam Aurangzeb Khan for all the wise words and kind prayers that have helped to make this book possible.

The publishers would like to thank the following for permission to use photographs:

Andes Press Agency/Carlos Reyes-Mayer, p. 45; Andes Press Agency/D&C Hill, p. 52; Andrew Egan, p. 8; Hutchison Picture Library/Edward Parker, p. 44; Hutchison Picture Library/Nigel Smith, p. 42; Hutchison Picture Library/Titus Moser, p. 15; Panos Pictures/Jeremy Hartley, pp. 47 and 48; Panos Pictures/Penny Tweedie, p. 51; Rex Features/Eastlight Vienna, p. 55; Science Photo Library/Celestial Image Co., p. 57; Science Photo Library/ESA/Photo Library International, p. 40; Science Photo Library/Peter Menzel, p. 56. All other photographs supplied by Peter Sanders.

The publishers have made every effort to contact copyright holders. However, if any material has been incorrectly acknowledged, the publishers would be pleased to correct this at the earliest opportunity.

Contents

An Introduction to Islam

In this section you will

- read about the nature and importance of faith and trust;
- learn about how Islam seeks to strengthen faith in Allah;
- read about the aims of Islam for all Muslims.

Standing before Allah in prayer

Faith and trust

The religion of **Islam** is based on **belief**. To believe in something requires **faith** and **trust**. Faith is often seen as the courage to accept the challenges of belief, and trust is the certainty that you won't be let down.

The people who follow Islam are called **Muslims.** The worldwide community of Muslims is known as the **ummah.** The idea of the ummah is that Islam is considered one large family, different in local culture and custom, but still united as one family in the eyes of Allah.

Islam teaches that no one is superior to another except if one is more faithful to Allah. Islam aims at the development of a united human society on Earth guided by the holy laws of Allah.

Allah

All Muslims have faith and trust in **Allah,** the Almighty God who created all things. For Muslims, Islam is more than just a series of beliefs, it is a complete way of life. They believe that not only has Allah created all things, but that Allah has also provided guidance to help all people live good lives. Therefore, to be a true Muslim means to accept Allah as the one true God and to submit to His will.

A Muslim family

The aims of Islam

Islam grants freedom of thought to all believers. It strives to free the soul from sin and wrong and to strengthen it with goodness and purity. This is so that people can live lives dedicated to doing their best in the eyes of Allah, on behalf of other people and for themselves. Islam also aims to free the human self from vanity and greed, from envy and tension, and from fear and insecurity. Islam, through submission to Allah, seeks to free people from the worship of false gods and base desires, unfolding before them the horizons of goodness and excellence. Islam fills the hearts of Muslims with fear of Allah, for Muslims the only God in this world as well as the hereafter.

Islam wants to see its followers as honest, dutiful, pious, kind-hearted, reliable, and sincere; this is achieved by a system of worship and duties.

Muslims are certain of their faith because Allah has told people about Himself over the centuries through holy people known as prophets. This is called revelation since Allah has used prophets to reveal something of Himself to people. The **Qur'an,** the Muslim holy book, mentions by name 25 prophets of Allah beginning with **Adam (pbuh)** and finishing with **Muhammad** (pbuh). (To show deep respect to the prophets, Muslims say, "peace be upon him" when they mention a prophet by name. Often, "(pbuh)" appears as a sign of respect after the mention of the names of any of the prophets of Allah. We will not repeat it every time in this book, but it should be understood.)

For Muslims, the last of the prophets was Muhammad, to whom Allah revealed the Qur'an, Allah's final message for the guidance of all.

Faith and trust— necessities of life

When you think about it, faith and trust are essential for our lives to function normally. We trust the electrical equipment in our homes, the cars and buses we ride in and, in particular, we trust the people around us. Our families and friends are important to us, but so are doctors, dentists, teachers, police, and fire and rescue services. We trust them all. For example, no one demands to see proof of a doctor's qualifications during a consultation or operation; we trust them.

Trust is therefore a very important part of human life. Without it, we would hardly get anything done because so much time would be spent doubting and questioning everything.

Some might argue that the only things that can be seen as absolutely certain are mathematical ideas, such as $2 + 2 = 4$. This is a fact and cannot be disputed. However, such a fact is of no use to us should we need to see the dentist or receive first aid. It is our experiences that form most of our judgments. If we have a good experience of something or someone, then we are most likely to trust it or them.

It is in this way that Muslims trust Allah and have faith in Him as their God. Their experience of the world that Allah has made gives Muslims cause to trust that Allah is a powerful and loving God, and they have faith that He will care for His people.

The Prophet Muhammad

In this section you will

● find out about the vocation (calling) of the prophet Muhammad;

● begin to understand the nature of the message Muhammad conveyed to the people of Mecca;

● read about how the calling of all Muslims is the Islamic ideal of leading a good life.

Muhammad's childhood

The prophet Muhammad was born in **Mecca** in 569 C.E. Mecca is in what is now the country of Saudi Arabia.

By the time he was eight, his parents and grandparents were dead. He went into the care of his uncle, **Abu Talib,** a man who was kind and generous. Abu Talib traveled the region meeting many different people and doing business with them. Muhammad would often accompany his uncle on his business journeys.

The prophet of Islam

The people of Mecca were very superstitious and had little understanding of Allah, so they put their faith in statues and lucky charms. Muhammad was not like the others. He was a man of deep faith and he prayed regularly. Gradually his spiritual meditation grew deeper and deeper. He would often isolate himself in a cave on **Jabal-un-Nur** (the Mountain of Light). There he would pray and meditate and share what little food he had with passersby.

When he was 40 years old, Muhammad was meditating one night when suddenly the angel **Jibril** (Gabriel) appeared before him in the cave. The **angel** told him that Allah had chosen him

as His final messenger to all mankind. The angel told him to recite (read out loud) the words on the cloth he was carrying and Muhammad, although he could not read before that night, recited the following verses:

"In the name of Allah, most gracious, most merciful.
Recite! In the name of your Lord Who has created;
He has created man from a clot.
Recite! And your Lord is most generous.
Who taught by the pen,
He has taught man that which he knew not."

Qur'an, surah 96: 1–5

Muhammad was awed by this incident and returned home dazed. He told **Khadijah,** his wife, what had happened to him. Muhammad thought that some evil spirit might be involved. Khadijah consoled him, telling him that, unlike most of the people of Mecca, he had always been generous and kind, and assured him that Allah would protect him against all evil. Muhammad's marriage to Khadijah was important because it provided him with the love and companionship he needed to support the mission Allah had assigned to him.

Soon, another revelation directed him to warn people against evil, to encourage them to worship no other gods but Allah, and to give up everything that could offend Allah:

"O you, enveloped in garments,
Arise and warn!
And magnify your Lord
And purify your garments and keep away from idols.
And give not a thing in order to have more
And be patient for the sake of your Lord."

Qur'an, surah 74: 1–7

Another revelation commanded him to proclaim his mission openly:

"Proclaim openly that which you are
    commanded, and
Turn away from the idolaters.
Truly We will suffice you against the scoffers."

Qur'an, surah 15: 94–5

To Muhammad, it was essential that the people
of Mecca heard the message of the one, true
God and accepted the will of Allah, changed
their ways, and led better lives. It was
Muhammad's task to deliver the message. He
did this by the example of his own life, which
Muslims call **Sunna.** Muslims try to follow
Sunna to live in accordance with the will of
Allah.

The chain of revelations from Allah continued
until the last one came, 23 years after the first:

"This day, I have perfected your religion for you
and completed My favor upon you and have
chosen for you Islam as your religion."

Quar'an, surah 5:3

After Muhammad's death all the revelations that
he had received from Allah were put together as
the Qur'an, the holy book of Islam.

The cave above Mecca

Muhammad's vocation

Muslims believe that Muhammad
received a vocation from Allah. This
vocation came in the form of a calling to
go out to the people of Mecca and tell
them to change their ways. Allah told
Muhammad to tell the people that they
must believe in the one, true God, and
that they should stop drinking, swearing,
and acting violently. Instead, they should
live peacefully and respectfully together.

It was obvious that this was not going to
be easy to do. However, Muhammad stuck
to his task because of his deep faith and
trust in Allah.

The vocation of every Muslim

Muslims believe that everyone has the
potential to receive a vocation from Allah.
It is true that not all callings are likely to
be as dramatic as the one that
Muhammad received, but all people can
accept the calling to serve God in some
way in their lives. This is because all the
good aspects of human life are seen as
aspects of Allah's love and creating power.
For example, Islam teaches that all people
have a calling to work hard, whether at
school, in a job, or around the house. We
are to develop our talents and skills so
that they may reflect the glory of Him
who gave them. Similarly, Allah calls all
people to marry and raise families who
know and love Him and follow His
commandments.

The Prophets

In this section you will

- learn the essential characteristics of a prophet;
- discover the importance of prophethood in Islam;
- learn how prophets of Judaism and Christianity are important to Muslims.

The messengers of Allah

Understanding the importance of prophethood is essential for a complete understanding of Islam. Muslims believe that a prophet is someone who is chosen by Allah to give guidance to other people. Some prophets receive messages or written revelation, as did Moses and Muhammad. In this way these prophets were **messengers.**

The word "messenger" comes from the Arabic word "**risalah,**" which means "message." In this case it means "prophecy," or the telling of important news.

Prophethood is not something that can be acquired by an individual's personal effort or devotion to Allah. It is a special gift that Allah gives to a human being. There is no human involvement in Allah's decision on who is fit to be a prophet.

In the **Qur'an** this calling from Allah is called **istifaa,** which means the selection of the best people. Muslims believe that the prophets, while fully human, were given special qualities by Allah in order to perform their missions.

	Qur'anic name	Biblical name
1	Adam	Adam
2	Idris	Enoch
3	Noh	Noah
4	Hud	——
5	Salih	——
6	Ibrahim	Abraham
7	Isma'il	Ishmael
8	Ishaq	Isaac
9	Lut	Lot
10	Ya'qub	Jacob
11	Yusuf	Joseph
12	Shu'aib	——
13	Ayyub	Job
14	Musa	Moses
15	Harun	Aaron
16	Dhul-Kifl	Ezekiel
17	Dawud	David
18	Suleiman	Solomon
19	Ilyas	Elias
20	Al Yasa'	Elisha
21	Yunus	Jonah
22	Zakaryah	Zechariah
23	Yahya	John
24	'Isa	Jesus
25	Muhammad	——

The prophets of Islam

The message

"A prophet never speaks on his own accord Nor does he speak of (his own) desire. It is only a revelation revealed (by Allah)."

Qur'an, surah 53: 3–4

This means that Allah's message cannot be influenced by the personal thoughts or desires of a prophet. When a prophet tells the word of Allah, it is as though Allah is speaking directly through him. Prophets not only transmit revelation from God, but they also have guiding words for their people.

Here are examples of non-revelation teaching:

"He is not a believer who eats his fill while his neighbor remains hungry by his side."

Muhammad

"There are many who fast during the day and pray all night, but they gain nothing but hunger and sleeplessness."

Muhammad

"I say to you, love God and love your neighbor as you love yourself."

'Isa—Jesus

"When you fast, wash your face and look happy, that your fasting may not be seen by men but by your Father who is in secret; and your Father who is in secret will reward you."

'Isa—Jesus

"The Lord is in His holy temple, the Lord's throne is in Heaven; the Lord is good, He loves good deeds; the upright shall see His face."

Dawud—David

"The righteous has enough to satisfy his appetite, but the belly of the wicked suffers want."

Suleiman—Solomon

Allah's prophets

Muslims believe that over the centuries Allah has sent prophets to reveal to people something of His divine nature and purpose. Of all the prophets, Muhammad is the most significant to Islam because he was the bearer of Allah's final message for humankind. However, the other prophets are very important too. Among these prophets are 'Isa (Jesus), Noh (Noah), and Ibrahim (Abraham).

The prophet 'Isa—Jesus

Christians believe that 'Isa (Jesus) was God's son. They believe that at the end of his earthly ministry 'Isa was put to death, crucified by the Roman authorities, and that after three days he was brought to life again in the resurrection. Although 'Isa is an important prophet for them, Muslims disagree with this understanding of his nature.

Islam teaches that the birth of 'Isa was a miracle. His mother was the virgin Maryam and he was conceived by the command of Allah (surah 19: 17–21). 'Isa was called to be a prophet when he was 30 years old, and he worked as a prophet for three years (surah 19: 29–34). Allah gave him miraculous powers: he could heal the sick, give sight to the blind and make the dead come back to life.

Islam contends that 'Isa called people to obey Allah alone but that some of his followers were so impressed by him that they considered him to be a part of Allah, the son of Allah (surah 5: 116–117). Muslims believe this to be an incorrect understanding of the person and work of 'Isa. Allah is one and indivisible. Allah can have no son or daughter, and to make such a claim implies a partnership. Islam states that Allah has no partners and to suggest that He has is a very grave sin (surah 5: 17, 19: 35).

The Qur'an teaches that the prophet 'Isa was not crucified. Rather, he was taken up into heaven by Allah and did not suffer a human death.

In this section you will

- learn about the role of the imam in the Muslim community;
- discover the important role learned people play in the faith of Islam;
- learn about the Islamic concept of Allah as a merciful God.

The role of the imam

Many world faiths depend on the work of local religious leaders to guide them in their spiritual development and to be available to advise or comfort them in particular times of crisis or need. For example, Jews may look to their rabbi or Christians to their minister or priest at such times. Jewish rabbis and Christian priests are often paid for the work they do since the calling to serve God that they are following is their full time occupation. The role of the **imam** in the Islamic community is different.

Generally speaking, in Islam there are no paid religious leaders. The **Qur'an** is clear in stating that Islam should not try to attract people to serve Allah by the promise of financial rewards.

"Leading a community in prayer before Allah is an honor, and teaching the meaning and importance of the word of Allah a privilege; to be paid would add nothing.

"I trained for seven years to become an imam. The training involved full study of both the Koran and the **Hadiths**. I felt called to this through a sense of wanting to develop my own prayer life and dedication to Allah. The honor of being asked to then help others is a great bonus. Allah has given all things, including all our feelings and emotions. One thing in particular that He has given is the ability to ask questions like, Who am I? Where have I come from? and, Where am I going? in terms of my relationship with Allah. I am a child of Allah and as such I want to grow closer to Him, fully engaged in His service.

"I see my main task as being there to help others to maintain their prayer life. For me my prayer life is rather like owning a car—if you look after it and service it regularly, it will serve you well. So it is with prayer. Looked after well, your prayer life will flourish and serve you well for life."

Imam Aurangzeb Khan

Imam Aurangzeb Khan

Although it is rare, Muslim scholars have stated that in certain circumstances where a man is dedicated and fully engaged in his work as an imam, then he may receive payment. The imam is usually chosen by the local Muslim community that he is to serve. Any Muslim of good character can be an imam providing he

- has a good knowledge of Islam;
- is respected and held in high regard by fellow Muslims;
- has studied the Qur'an, the holy book of Islam, and the Hadiths, and the sayings of the prophet Muhammad, in Arabic, and understands them well.

An imam leading worship in a mosque

● is known for his faithfulness to and love of Allah and his ability to make wise decisions based on good judgment.

Leading prayers

The main role of the imam is to lead the prayers at the **mosque** (the local center of Muslim worship, and also called "masjid," or place of prostration) in his community. Before the Friday lunchtime prayers (the special weekly communal prayers) the imam will give two short talks or sermons called the **khutbah.** These sermons will usually involve an explanation of verses of the Koran or else a consideration of the important relevance of the Hadiths for Muslims today.

Similarly, it is the imam who often leads prayers and reads the sermon at a Muslim marriage or funeral. He also takes a leading role in the work of the **madrasah,** or school, at the mosque where young Muslims go to study Islam, in particular the Qur'an, and to learn Arabic.

It is essential to remember that the imam is not a leader of Muslims. Islam is a faith that allows all its followers to worship Allah for themselves. No Muslim, however learned or pious, would ever tell another what to do or how to live, because Muslims believe that we are all ultimately answerable to Allah alone as individuals. The imam, however, always encourages all in his community to live their lives in accordance with Islamic teachings.

Some Muslim prayers

After leading the community in prayer at the mosque, the imam will often make his own personal prayers to Allah. Often, the opportunity will be taken to ask Allah for forgiveness and mercy for all the times His high expectations have not been met.

The concept of Allah as a merciful and compassionate God is very powerful. Despite being hurt by human arrogance and sinfulness, Allah will always grant forgiveness and another chance to all those who call upon Him.

"In fact there is no real need to say such prayers out loud. Allah knows all the secrets of every heart and so will have forgiven the person who is truly sorry even before they voice their prayer."

Imam Aurangzeb Khan

Such prayers can be said either in Arabic (the language of the Qur'an) or in the individual's own language.

"O our Lord, grant us good in this world and good in the next world, save us from the punishment of hell."

"O Allah, you are the source of peace …, you are most highly exalted, O lord of majesty and honor."

"O Allah, forgive me and my parents and my teachers and all believing men and women and all Muslim men and women in your great mercy. O most merciful lord, you have all mercy."

"Our lord, we have wronged ourselves. Forgive us and have mercy on us. Without you we cannot win through."

Muslim Beliefs

In this section you will

● find out about the most important Islamic beliefs;

● read about the five pillars, or supporting beliefs, of Islam.

Muslims believe that the religion of Islam, as revealed to the **prophet** Muhammad, is the true religion of Allah, the one true God. The most fundamental **beliefs** of Islam are:

1. in Allah
2. in the will of Allah
3. in the angels of Allah
4. in the books of Allah
5. in the messengers (prophets) of Allah
6. in the day of judgment
7. in life after death

These seven fundamental beliefs can be placed into three broader groups:

1. **Tawhid**—the oneness of Allah
2. **Risalah**—the work and message of the prophets
3. **Akhirah**—life after death

Tawhid, Risalah, and Akhirah summarize all of the Muslim way of life.

Tawhid

Tawhid means the oneness of Allah. It is the main part of the faith of Muslims and is expressed in the **Qur'an**:

"Say, He is Allah, the One. Allah is the self-sufficient master whom all creatures need. He begets not nor was begotten. And there is none equal or comparable to Him."

Qur'an, surah 112

Tawhid means that everything on earth is created by Allah. It is Allah who is, therefore, the sustainer of the universe and the only source of human guidance.

Risalah

Risalah refers to the important role played by the prophets in Islam.

"Allah sent among them a messenger from among themselves, reciting unto them His verses, and purifying them, and instructing them in the book and wisdom."

Qur'an, surah 3: 164

Akhirah

Akhirah refers to the important Muslim belief in a life after death that can be enjoyed by all believers. Allah's message is:

2

3. ANGELS OF ALLAH
4. BOOKS OF ALLAH
5. MESSENGERS OF ALLAH

RISALAH

1

1. ALLAH
2. WILL OF ALLAH

TAWHID

3

6. DAY OF JUDGMENT
7. LIFE AFTER DEATH

AKHIRAH

"Did you think that we had created you in play and that you would not be brought back to us?'

Qur'an, surah 23: 115

Another way to view the faith of Islam is contained in the **Hadith** of Gabriel:

"We were sitting with Allah's Messenger, [and] a man suddenly appeared before us … and said: 'O Muhammad, tell me about Islam.' Allah's Messenger said: 'Islam is to bear witness that there is no god except Allah and that Muhammad is the Messenger of Allah, and to establish regular [habits of doing Islamic duty]' …. He then said: 'Tell me about Iman—Belief. 'The Prophet said: 'Iman is to believe in Allah, His Angels, His Books, His Messengers, the Last Day, and to believe in Divine Preordainment.… He then said: 'Tell me about Ihsan—Excellence (virtue).' He said: 'Ihsan is to worship Allah as if you saw Him [because] He sees you.' …Then the stranger went away. The Prophet…said, 'This was Gabriel; he came to teach you your religion.'"

Sharia—Islamic law

Sharia is the entire body of Islamic law, which has been put together from four sources that are generally recognized as Islamic authorities:

1. The Qur'an;
2. The example of Muhammad's life—Sunna;
3. Consensus (general agreement)—ijma;
4. Analogical reasoning—qiyas.

Islam not only directs Muslims to follow Allah's word in the Qur'an, but it also combines interpretation and experience as part of the law.

There are five categories of acts in Islamic law. Any given act will fall in one of these categories.

1. Obligatory—Neglect brings punishment (this world and next); doing them is rewarded; for example, The Five Pillars.
2. Recommended—Reward for doing; no punishment for not doing; for example, optional prayers; pious deeds.
3. Indifferent/permissible—No reward or punishment either way. Countless things we do every day are in this category.
4. Reprehensible/discouraged—No punishment for doing; reward for avoiding; for example, divorce or polygamy.
5. Forbidden—Punishment for doing; reward for refraining; for example, theft, wine drinking.

One question in Islamic countries today is whether they should be guided by sharia, or have a separate constitution, leaving adherence to sharia to the private lives of Muslims.

The duty to worship Allah

There are five important parts to Muslim worship. Together they could be said to support or "hold up" what it means to be a Muslim. They are known as the five pillars of Islam.

The first pillar is shahadah, what every Muslim believes: that there is only one God—Allah—and that Muhammad is His prophet. It belongs at the very heart of every Muslim act of worship.

The second pillar is salah, prayer five times a day. This is the clearest evidence of the worship that Muslims offer to Allah.

The third pillar is zakah, giving money or "alms" to people who are poor or needy. This is a powerful form of worship, because through helping other people Allah is being served.

The fourth pillar is sawm, fasting (going without food) during the month of Ramadan. Fasting is a form of worship because it helps to focus hearts and minds on Allah and the needs of others.

The fifth pillar is **Hajj**, pilgrimage to Mecca. This is the most holy of all places on Earth for Muslims.

Allah

In this section you will

- learn about the most important characteristics of Allah;
- learn how people have tried to describe God;
- read some of the many names used for God in Islam.

Islamic beliefs about Allah

Some people seem to live their entire lives without ever thinking about the reason for their existence, or whether there is any point to their lives, or any goal to be aimed for. Many think there is a universe and that is all there is. They believe their lives are simply a chain of events until they die.

Muslims, however, say it is impossible for anything to have being or purpose without God. To recognize that Allah does exist and is the beginning and end of all things is essential to the faith of Islam.

Muslims believe that Allah is one, that Allah creates and sustains all things and that there is no other god except Him. This belief is called tawhid. The prophet Muhammad strongly opposed to all forms of belief in God that denied His oneness and unity.

The word "Islam" means "submission." The way in which Muslims submit themselves to the will of Allah accurately reflects what Muslims believe about Allah and the way in which Allah expects them to live their lives. True Muslims would never put themselves and what they want first, but reflect on what Allah would expect and obey what they believe is His will.

Allah, the name of God

Shirk

Blasphemy means acting or speaking disrespectfully about God. The Arabic word **shirk** describes a form of blasphemy.

Shirk means the blasphemy of "association." This means to talk or act in any way that denies that Allah is Lord over everything, by associating Him with someone or something else. Anyone who does this commits the most awful blasphemy. The name "Allah" in Arabic—the language of the **Qur'an**—has no plural form, and is neither male nor female. Shirk, then, is either the worship of anything other than Allah, or the association of Allah with anything other than Allah.

Why do you think Muslims might feel the power of Allah is displayed in this sunrise?

Understanding Allah

Muslims often understand Allah best in terms of the wonders of His creation. The whole universe is Allah's creation and everything in it belongs to Allah and is dependent on Allah.

"Allah alone created all things, gave all things … Allah is like nothing or no one. Allah is greater than anything we can ever hope to imagine. It's pointless and wrong to ever try to bring Allah down to our level. The love and power of Allah is a beautiful mystery. I'm happy with that."

Mariah, aged 14

One of the best ways to understand the way Muslms think of the power of Allah in the universe is through an appreciation of the light that Allah has provided for the world. The following quotations show how important the gift of light is for Muslims.

"Allah will give you a light by which you will walk."

Qur'an, surah 57: 28

"O Lord! Illuminate my heart with light, my sight with light, and my hearing with light. Let there be light on my right hand and on my left, and light behind me, and light going before me."

A prayer of Muhammad

"O God, who knows the innermost secrets of our hearts—lead us out of the darkness into the light."

A prayer of Muhammad

Names of Allah

Muslims have 99 names for Allah, which express His nature in all its diversity. Here are the first 33 of Allah's names:

God
The Compassionate
The Merciful
The King
The Holy
The Peace
The One with Faith
The Protector
The Mighty
The Repairer
The Imperious
The Creator
The Maker
The Fashioner
The Forgiver
The Dominant
The Bestower
The Provider
The Opener
The Knower
The Contractor
The Expander
The Humbler
The Exalter
The Honourer
The Abaser
The Hearer
The Seer
The Judge
The Just
The Subtle
The Aware
The Gentle

Thinking About Allah

In this section you will

● read about why it is not easy to talk about Allah;

● see how language can be developed that enables people to reflect on the nature and being of Allah.

Madrasah—"Muslim children learning ways to effectively express their beliefs about Allah"

The nature of the universe

For some people understanding the nature of Allah is difficult. People traditionally tend to think of Allah as being "up there,"

A depiction of the universe in three parts

inhabiting a wonderful place called Heaven, surrounded by His **angels** and all the good people who have died and gone to glory. The opposite is said about **Shaytan** (the Devil), who dwells far "beneath the earth" in Hell, surrounded by the forces of evil and all the wicked people who are being punished for their sins after their death. This would mean that we as human beings inhabit some kind of middle ground, called Earth.

Of course we now know scientifically that the universe in which we live is not like that. Still, people need to talk about things in familiar ways that they can understand. So we may point to the sky and say it is "up," when we know that this seems true to us only because our feet are held to the earth by the force of gravity.

The nature of Allah

While it is impossible to conceive of Allah, He reveals a number of divine attributes and names so that we humans, with our physical bodies, can call upon Him. The order of the universe and the beauty of creation reflect some of Allah, and we can know from these things that Allah is great, but we cannot attempt to describe what is beyond language or see what is beyond our senses. Islam, in fact, forbids any visual representations of Allah, because Allah cannot be limited (to a picture, a statue, or a word).

The beauty of Allah's creation

Muslims often refer to Allah as "He" or things belonging to Allah as "His." This does not mean that Allah is male or that Allah is not female. It gives human beings, who can only have a limited understanding of Allah and a limited vocabulary, a way to refer to Allah in prayer, other forms of worship, and expression of religious feelings.

The 99 names of Allah

Understanding Allah— a parable

The concept of God is not an easy one to either understand or explain. This parable, although not Islamic in origin, can help us to understand what Muslims mean when they talk of their faith and trust in Allah.

A 19th-century British clergyman and scientist named William Paley compared God to a watchmaker, to prove God's existence.

"In crossing a heath, suppose I pitched my foot against a stone, and were asked how the stone came to be there; I might possibly answer that, for anything I knew to the contrary, it had lain there forever…. But suppose I had found a watch upon the ground, and it should be inquired how the watch happened to be in that place; I should hardly think of the answer I had given before, that for anything I knew, the watch might always have been there."

Paley goes on to describe the inner working of a clock, the intricately arranged cogs and springs. He then says that the intricacy of design forces us to conclude "that the watch must have had a maker, that there must have existed, at some time…an artificer or artificers, who formed it for [a] purpose…who comprehended its construction, and designed its use."

Paley suggests that we must do the same when we observe the intricacies and complexities of nature. Just as the amazing design of the watch makes us to believe in a watchmaker, so the amazing design of creation leads us to believe in a "Divine Watchmaker," God.

Signs and Symbols

Muslims feel little need for symbols in their religion. However, as a reminder of the guidance Allah provides for His people, two very powerful symbols are often used in Islam.

The star and crescent moon

Islam began in the desert of Arabia among nomadic farmers who would travel by night, away from the searing heat of the sun's rays, in search of the best food and water for their animals. The moon would provide light through the darkness of the night and the stars gave fixed points which the people could use to navigate the vast desert. In the same way, Muslims think of Allah as the great guiding light in their lives.

Islam teaches that Allah has revealed the truth through the prophet Muhammad as a guide for life, for all humanity, and for all time. The star and crescent moon provide a reminder for Muslims of both the permanence and the benefits of the word and will of Allah.

"Allah is the Spirit, the power behind all things. Allah is in all things."

Salim, aged 13

"I know that Allah loves all that He has made. Best of all Allah loves us, so we return love in worship."

Mariah, aged 14

"Allah is every mystery and every answer in the universe."

Mudassir, aged 15

Religious language

The need for symbolic language in religion is important. When you think of it, we expect our language to cover a vast range of different jobs. Sometimes it may be used to portray feelings of love or other emotions. At other times it may be used to teach complex mathematics, comfort an upset child, or negotiate a business deal. We require our language to cover a wide range of emotions and situations. Unfortunately, we only have a limited vocabulary, so we tend to use the same word for a variety of meanings. For example, the word "love":

1. Janet loves strawberries.
2. Janet loves her mom and dad.
3. Janet loves her cuddly teddy bear.

It is not easy to gain an exact understanding of a word as popular as "love" since it can mean different things to different people at different times.

When people want to talk about God, they have to use everyday language. There is a problem, therefore, in what is meant exactly by "God is good" or "God loves us." Things to be aware of when addressing this problem include:

1. a. Religious language, talk about God, is used in a special way since it is describing something unique;

   b. Religious language is used in a very specific sense and should not be confused with the everyday language of the home, school, and playground.

2. It is because of the difficulties presented by the use of everyday words to express religious truths that symbols, analogies, and myths are used widely by people of many religions to express their beliefs about God.

   a. symbols—pictures with a powerful meaning;

   b. analogies, "symbolic pictures"—"drawn" with words describing what something could be said to be like. For example, "Allah's love for us is like the love of a parent for a child";

   c. myths—stories that share with the reader important religious truths.

Allah in the Qur'an

"Allah is the Light of the heavens and the earth. The similitude of His light is as a niche wherein is a lamp. The lamp is in a glass. The glass is as it were a shining star. (This lamp is) kindled from a blessed tree, an olive neither of the East nor of the West, whose oil would almost glow forth (of itself) though no fire touched it. Light upon light. Allah guideth unto His light whom He will. And Allah speaketh to mankind in allegories, for Allah is Knower of all things."

Qur'an, surah 24:35

Translation by Marmaduke Pickthall, from *The Meaning of the Glorious Qur'an*

Symbolism and decoration in Islam

Symbolism is important in Islam, as it is in most religions. The star and crescent moon are thought of as the symbols of Islam. They are good representations of the way Muslims perceive Allah. Islam has no real need for any other symbols.

However, Muslims have developed a beautiful style of art to decorate mosques and editions of the Qur'an, using a variety of geometric designs and patterns. No depictions of humans or animals are allowed, since, according to Muhammad, only Allah can make living things and to try to imitate Allah would be sinful.

Worship—Shahadah

The five pillars of Islam

The most important duty of every Muslim is to worship Allah. The word "worship" in English comes from a very old word meaning "to give worth." It is clear in this case that Allah is "worth" a great deal of praise and adoration, worthy of and demanding the complete submission of His people to His will.

Worshiping Allah, then, demands the total obedience of every Muslim to follow His commands and to do His will. The Arabic word for such obedience in worship is **ibadah.** Ibadah comes from the Arabic word **abd,** which means servant or slave. A servant or slave is someone who is completely obedient to his or her master. Every Muslim would happily admit that Allah alone is their Lord and master.

"It is then as Allah's servant or slave, that Muslims try to live their life. In doing so every aspect of their life is the worship of Allah, from working to relaxing, from praying to raising a family."

Imam Aurangzeb Khan

There are five duties that are of fundamental importance in Muslim worship. These five duties, often referred to as "pillars," include:

1 **shahadah**—the declaration of faith in Allah;

2 **salah**—prayer five times each day;

3 **zakah**—the giving of money for the poor;

4 **sawm**—fasting during the month of Ramadan;

5 **Hajj**—pilgrimage to Mecca at least once in a lifetime.

Shahadah

The first and most important duty of every Muslim is to declare faith in Allah. Islam teaches that, to make this declaration, a person must proclaim with the lips and believe in the heart:

"Ash-hadu an la ilaha ill-Allah wa ash-hadu anna Muhammadar Rasulullah."
("I bear witness that there is no other god but Allah; and I bear witness that Muhammad is the messenger of Allah.")

The first part of this declaration has two aspects, one positive and one negative. "There is no other god" is the negative aspect, "but Allah" is the positive aspect affirming for the Muslim the truth and certainty of Allah.

The saying of these Arabic words is called **shahadah,** the declaration of faith. The shahadah is repeated by Muslims every day during each of the five required prayer times. The words form the heart of the Muslim call to prayer (the **adhan**), used to summon Muslims to prayer five times each day. The call to prayer is also the first words whispered into the ear of a newborn baby. Similarly, the last words uttered by a Muslim before dying should ideally be the **Kalimah Tayyibah,** which, like the call to prayer, summarizes the Muslim belief that Allah is one and that Muhammad is his messenger.

"The message of Islam is very important and very simple, because if Allah wants you to do something He lets you know. The prophet has taught that Allah wants worship, our way of thanking Him for everything. This worship is in the five pillars. You make a choice, to follow and worship Allah or not. It's a way of choosing either Heaven (being with Allah) or Hell (being separated from Allah).

"Islam means to submit yourself, give in to Allah. Worshiping Allah involves time and commitment throughout your life. It is right to worship. Look at everything we have been given by Allah."

Shamira, aged 13

The adhan

Islam encourages Muslims to say their compulsory prayers in the mosque whenever possible. To call Muslims to prayer, the prophet Muhammad introduced the **adhan**—the call to prayer. The person who recites the adhan is called the mu'adhin (muezzin). He stands in the minaret of the mosque, faces Mecca, raises his hands to his ears and calls out a special formula of words.

The words of the adhan

During the call to prayer, the Mu'adhin will call out these words:

Allahu Akbar
Allahu Akbar
Allahu Akbar
Allahu Akbar
Ash-hadu an la ilaha ill-Allah
Ash -hadu an la ilaha ill-Allah
Ash-hadu anna Muhammadar Rasulullah
Ash-hadu anna Muhammadar Rasulullah
Hayya 'alas salah
Hayya 'alas salah
Hayya 'alal falah
Hayya 'alal falah
Allahu Akbar
Allahu Akbar
la ilaha ill-Allah

This may be translated as:

Allah is the greatest
Allah is the greatest
Allah is the greatest
Allah is the greatest
I bear witness that there is no god but
    Allah
I bear witness that there is no god but
    Allah
I bear witness that Muhammad is Allah's
    messenger
I bear witness that Muhammad is Allah's
    messenger
Rush to prayer
Rush to prayer
Rush to success
Rush to success
Allah is the greatest
Allah is the greatest
There is no god but Allah

Worship—Salah 1

Salah

Salah is one of the most important of the five basic duties of Islam since it requires Muslims to focus their hearts and minds completely on Allah in prayer five times every day. The way in which Muslims pray is found in the **Sunna** of Muhammad, and the times at which prayers are said are laid out in the **Qur'an.** Muslims can come closer to Allah by performing salah regularly, correctly, and with a full understanding of its significance and meaning.

Muslims believe that the purpose of human creation is to worship Allah. Allah declares in the Qur'an:

"And I created not … mankind except that they worship me."

Qur'an, surah 51:56

Therefore, Muslims believe that whatever we do, we must bear in mind that we are doing it for Allah's sake. Only then can we expect to gain any benefit from the performance of salah.

"Salah is important for a number of reasons.

- It brings men and women closer to Allah.
- It keeps human beings away from forbidden activities.

Muslims at prayer

- It is designed to control evil desires and passions.
- It purifies the heart, develops the mind, and comforts the soul.
- It is a constant reminder of Allah and His greatness.
- It develops discipline and willpower.
- It shows that Islam is one universal family—the ummah.
- It is a means of cleanliness, purity, and punctuality.
- It develops gratitude, humility, and refinement.
- It is a sign of total obedience to the will of Allah.

"Similarly, the Qur'an teaches that if your salah does not improve the way in which you conduct your life, you must think seriously and find out where you are going wrong."

Imam Aurangzeb Khan

The times of salah

Salah is performed five times every day at special times:

1 Salat-ul-fajr—between first light and sunrise;

2 Salat-ul-zuhr—just after the sun has left its highest point in the sky;

3 Salat-ul-asr—between midafternoon and sunset;

4 Salat-ul-maghrib—between sunset and darkness;

5 Salat-ul-isha—between darkness and dawn.

Rak'ahs

Salah is performed by following a strict ritual of set movements and prayers. A rak'ah is a sequence of movements. Two rak'ahs are repeated at Salat-ul-Fajr; four at Salat-ul-Zuhr and Salat-ul-Asr; three at Salat-ul-Maghrib; and four at Salat-ul-Isha. At each rak'ah, set prayers are repeated.

Eight positions make up a rak'ah:

1 standing up straight;

2 raising your hands to your ears;

3 placing your right hand on your left hand just below your navel or on your chest;

4 bowing down;

5 placing your hands on your knees;

6 prostrating yourself with your forehead, nose, palms of your hands, and knees touching the floor;

7 kneeling upright;

8 while still kneeling, turning your face from left to right.

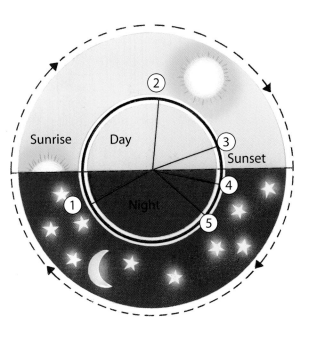

Worship—Salah 2

In this section you will

● read about the preparations made by Muslims before they pray;

● learn how Muslims value focusing the heart and mind before praying;

● find out about the different ways in which Muslims pray.

Preparing for salah

"Islam requires Muslims to pray five times every day.

"Before we say salah, we prepare ourselves. In order to focus our hearts and minds on Allah, before prayer we wash. This is called **wudu.** Wudu is compulsory and we cannot make our salah without first making our wudu.

"Wudu, like salah, is written in the Koran. It requires the washing of different parts of our bodies, even if we are not very dirty. It is more of a spiritual washing as we prepare to stand before Allah."

Imam Aurangzeb Khan

Muslims follow a set pattern or ritual after entering into a prayerful frame of mind. They dedicate the wudu that they are about to perform "in the name of Allah, the most merciful, the most kind." The wudu rituals, in order, are:

● The hands are washed up to the wrists three times;

● the mouth is rinsed three times;

● the nostrils are washed three times, and so is the tip of the nose;

● the face is washed thoroughly three times;

● both arms are washed up to the elbow three times;

A Muslim performing wudu

● wet hands are then passed over the hair from the forehead to the neck;

● wet hands are run over the ears and neck;

● both feet are washed up to the ankles.

In addition to the daily salah obligations, Muslims can also make their own private and personal prayers at any time. This type of prayer is called **nafl.** Nafl also provides the opportunity to meditate on the wonderful gifts Allah has given or to seek the strength of Allah to work hard in their religious duties and to become better people.

Prayers called **du'a** are an opportunity for every Muslim to bring before Allah his or her own individual concerns; for example, to pray for someone who is ill or has a particular need.

Du'a prayer

Therefore, different types of prayer can be included in the performance of du'a. These may include:

- intercession—praying for the needs of others;

- supplication—asking for the strength to overcome the temptations and pressures of the world and to grow in faith;

- confession—saying you're sorry before Allah for the times when the temptations to sin have been too strong to resist.

Set prayers at salah

Set prayers are repeated at salah, accompanying the different positions which make up a rak'ah. It is very important for Muslims to follow the correct procedure. These are some of the prayers recited at salah.

"Allah is the greatest."

"O Allah, glory and praise are for you, and blessed is your name, and exalted is your majesty: you alone are God."

"I seek shelter in Allah from Shaytan."

"In the name of Allah, the most merciful, the most kind."

"Glory to you my Lord, the great."

"Allah hears those who praise Him."

"Praise to you, our Lord."

"Glory to you my Lord, the highest."

"Peace and mercy of Allah be upon you."

The opening chapter of the **Qur'an** is always recited during salah, and a further passage is also selected and read out.

"All praise be to Allah,
the Lord of the Universe,
the Most Merciful, the Most Kind,
Master of the Day of Judgment.
You alone do we worship,
From you alone do we seek help.
Show us the straight path, the way
of those earning Your favor.
Keep us from the path of
those earning Your anger,
those who are going astray."

Qur'an, surah 1

Worship—Sawm

In this section you will

● learn the importance of fasting in the lives of Muslims;

● read about ways in which fasting can strengthen people in faith as well as self-discipline;

● learn more about traditional practices during the month of Ramadan.

Sawm

Sawm is the fourth pillar of Islam. Sawm means "fasting" and all adult Muslims must fast from dawn to sunset every day of **Ramadan,** the ninth month of the Islamic calendar. In practice this means abstaining from eating, drinking, smoking, and sexual relations during the hours of daylight. Travelers, pregnant women, and those who are ill during Ramadan can put off not eating and drinking and make up for it later.

Sawm can develop self-control and help people to overcome selfishness, greed, and laziness. It is in effect an annual opportunity to refresh and refocus the hearts and minds of Muslims in their worship of Allah.

By fasting Muslims experience for themselves what it is like to have an empty stomach. This develops an empathy for all the poor and hungry people in the world. Fasting teaches Muslims to control the love of comfort. It also helps Muslims to control sexual desires. The **Qur'an** is clear in its teaching that eating, comfort, and sex are three things that must be kept under control to behave effectively as Allah's servants:

"O you who believe! Fasting is prescribed for you, as it was prescribed for those before you, that you may become pious."

Qur'an, surah 2: 183

A Muslim family breaking the fast

Fasting, therefore, is a sign of a truly obedient Muslim. The following actions, however, break the rules of fast:

1 deliberate eating or drinking

2 anything entering the body through the nose or mouth; this includes smoking

3 having any sexual relations

Muslims are expected to make an extra effort to refrain from all immoral actions during the fast. They try not to tell lies, break a promise, or do anything deceitful.

The importance of sawm

The purpose of fasting is to help make Muslims able to control passions and desires so that they become people of good deeds and intentions. Similarly, fasting helps to develop an increased awareness of knowing what it is like to go without, even for a little while, and to know hunger.

Exceptions to the rule

Although most Muslims can and will take part in fasting during Ramadan, there are sometimes unavoidable circumstances that mean a person is unable to fast.

Very young children and the elderly are not expected to fast at all, and neither are women who are pregnant. If a Muslim is ill or is traveling during Ramadan, he or she is excused from fasting at that time, but is expected to make up for any missed days later.

At the end of Ramadan, Muslims celebrate with a day of thanksgiving and happiness. The festival of **Id-ul-Fitr** is one of the great occasions for the Muslim community. On this day Muslims offer special prayers at the mosque and thank Allah for all His blessings and mercies.

In addition to the mandatory fasting in Ramadan, Muslims may fast during other times of the year in order to refocus their hearts and minds on Allah.

Worship during Ramadan

The month of Ramadan is very important to Muslims. It is the month in which the Qur'an was first revealed to the prophet Muhammad.

During the month of Ramadan there is one night, which to Muslims is "better than a thousand months" (Qur'an surah 97: 3). This night is called Lailatul Qadr (the Night of Power) and it falls, according to the **Hadiths**, during the last ten days of the month. Many Muslims will pass this night in worship for as long as they can.

During the month of Ramadan additional prayers are repeated during salah. Tarawih is a special prayer through which Muslims attempt to recite as much of the Qur'an as possible. In many mosques, the whole of the Qur'an is recited through Tarawih prayer. Although usually recited by the congregation at the mosque, any Muslim who cannot attend the mosque should try to say Tarawih at home.

The Mosque

In this section you will

- read about the Muslim place of worship;
- learn the variety of ways the mosque is used by Muslims;
- read about the decorations that adorn the mosques, and rules about them.

The importance of the mosque

Muslims believe that Allah can be worshiped anywhere. The prophet Muhammad said:

"When the hour of prayer overtakes you, you shall perform it, because the whole earth has been turned into a mosque for me."

Hadith

However, most Muslim communities have a special building set aside for worship, called a **mosque.** Mosques are important because they provide essential facilities for local people to pray.

The main features of a mosque include:

- the main prayer hall;
- a separate section in which women pray;
- a domed ceiling symbolizing the heavens above;
- a **minaret:** a tower from which the community is called to prayer five times each day;
- a **minbar:** a raised platform;
- a **mihrab:** an archway showing the exact direction of Mecca.

In addition, all mosques have a supply of running water, and separate rooms for women and men to place their shoes and to perform **wudu.**

Custom-built mosques often include offices and a number of rooms used for a variety of community needs, including:

- the mosque school where Muslim children can learn Arabic and more about their faith (the madrasah);
- a room for celebrations and parties;
- courts to hear cases relating to Islamic law.

Prayers are said five times every day at the mosque and are led by the imam. At the main Friday prayers, the imam will speak from the minbar and give sermons explaining the meaning and importance of the **Hadiths**—the sayings of the prophet Muhammad —or the **surahs** (chapters) of the **Qur'an.**

A mosque in Jeddah, Saudi Arabia

"The mosque is important as a focus of community prayer and learning, but, for me, not as important as my own family as the heart of my religion. The mosque is used regularly, every day, for people to go and pray to Allah and to learn new things, every day of your life. I have spent time at the mosque **madrasah** for seven years. I started when I was four, and finished when I was ten."

Shamira, aged 13

"The most important prayers at the mosque are the Friday lunchtime prayers. I think Friday is important, as it shows Islam is separate from other religions; Judaism has Saturday, and Christianity Sunday."

Mudassir, aged 15

Inside the Niujie Mosque, the oldest mosque in Beijing, China

Calligraphy

Muslim artists often draw beautiful flowers and plants. A highly developed art form in Islam, however, is calligraphy—the art of handwriting.

Calligraphy is often used to write out passages from the Qur'an. To write out the surahs in this way honors the words of Allah and is a wonderful privilege for the artist writing them.

Calligraphy is also used to create beautiful pictures, made up of letters, words from the Qur'an and prayers. It can be used on pottery and tiles, as well as on paper. It is in this way that all mosques have been decorated to the glory of Allah over the centuries.

Beautiful mosques

The mosque is the place where Muslims meet to stand together before Allah in prayer. Mosques are usually beautifully decorated. They may have richly colored and patterned carpets and tiles, intricate stonework and chandeliers. However, the art and decorations which Muslims use in mosques are quite special.

Muhammad told his friends not to draw pictures of animals or people. He said that only Allah can make living beings, and it is wrong for human beings to try to imitate this.

Muhammad was also afraid that if people were to look at pictures or statues they might begin to worship them. Included in this were pictures or statues that were supposed to look like Allah or even Muhammad. Worshiping such objects would be idol worship. Idol worship is wrong because the Qur'an teaches that Muslims should only worship that which is perfect. Only Allah is perfect.

In this section you will
- find out about the importance of the Qur'an for Muslims;
- read about how the Qur'an is used by Muslims in worship.

The Qur'an: the word of Allah

Islam teaches that human beings are the servants of Allah. This is seen as a great responsibility, so Muslims believe that they need guidance to carry out their duties as Allah's servants. Islam teaches that humans are unable to guide themselves because they have many weaknesses and are frail and short-sighted. Muslims believe only Allah is above all things and that it is He alone who has the power to give guidance that works at all times and in all places. Therefore, He has sent prophets and messengers to show humanity the right path in life. In addition to this, He has also given holy books for guidance.

"Allah's favors and blessings are countless. He provides us with all that we need. However, Allah's greatest favor is His guidance contained in the books of revelation. The pure, perfect, and most useful knowledge comes only from Allah."

Imam Aurangzeb Khan

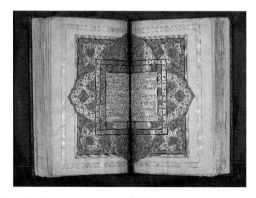

The Qur'an—the word of Allah

The books of Allah

Muslims believe that Allah has inspired all the books that are mentioned in the Koran. These include the **Tawrah** (Torah) of **Musa** (Moses), the **Zabur** (Psalms) of **Dawud** (David), the **Injil** (Gospel) of **'Isa** (Jesus), and the Koran revealed to Muhammad. The Qur'an also mentions the **Sohaf of Ibrahim** (Scrolls of Abraham).

Muslims believe that, of all the divine books, only the Qur'an exists in its original, unchanged form. The Zabur, Tawrah, and Injil were gradually altered after the death of the prophets to whom they were revealed, and their message is changed and distorted. In effect, they became a mixture of divine words with those of human beings.

Together, all these writings make up one divine revelation, although Islam teaches that the Qur'an is most important for guiding human actions. Through these holy writings, Allah has shown human beings something of His nature and has told them about the way in which He expects them to live their lives.

The message of the Qur'an

"The message of the Qur'an is valid for all times and conditions. This is because the Qur'an contains the original message revealed to Muhammad. This message, passed from mouth to mouth and from heart to heart for over 1,400 years, has enabled Muslims to know the true word of Allah."

Imam Aurangzeb Khan

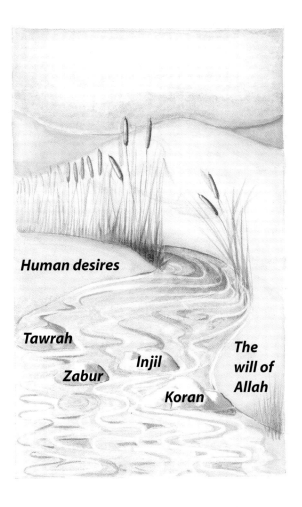

Human desires

Tawrah

Zabur

Injil

Koran

The will of Allah

Words from the Qur'an

Here are some passages taken from the Muslim holy book, the Qur'an.

"God chooses for Himself whoever He pleases, and guides to Himself those who turn (to Him)."

Qur'an, surah 42:13

"O people of the Book, you have no ground to stand on unless you stand fast by the Law, the Gospel, and all the revelation that came to you from God."

Qur'an, surah 5:68

"This is My straight path, so follow it, and do not follow paths that will separate you from this path."

Qur'an, surah 15:3

"He will provide for you a light by which you will walk; He will forgive, for God always forgives and is most merciful."

Qur'an, surah 57:28

Respecting the Qur'an

Muslims treat the Qur'an with tremendous respect and honor. There are strict guidelines about how to do this.

The Qur'an is never allowed to touch the ground, and nothing should ever be placed on top of it. Before reading it, Muslims wash or bathe very carefully.

Muslims never handle the Qur'an unnecessarily. While reading it, they do not speak, eat, or drink. When they put it away, they keep it covered to protect it from dust.

Holy Books—Hadiths

In this section you will

● learn how Muslims use the teachings of the prophet Muhammad;

● read about the importance of Muhammad as an example to Muslims;

● read about how truth as found in the Qur'an is interpreted by diferent schools of thought.

The importance of the Hadiths

Hadiths are important to Muslims. They are a collection of the words and teachings of the prophet Muhammad and are used by Muslims as a means of guidance and encouragement in their lives. This means that if ever faced with a difficult decision or dilemma, a Muslim can seek the help of Allah through the advice of the prophet Muhammad in the words of the Hadiths.

"No Muslim can underestimate the importance and significance of the Prophet. It was through him that Allah chose to finally reveal Himself, both in the words of the **Qur'an** and in the divine messages revealed though the Hadiths."

Imam Aurangzeb Khan

Hadiths are used by Muslims to help them live good lives. They provide guidance for living and can be applied to a wide range of social issues and situations.

Examples of Hadiths

1 "The best house among the Muslims is the house in which an orphan is well treated, and the worst house among the Muslims is the house in which an orphan is badly treated."

"One who tries to help the widow and the poor is like a warrior in the way of Allah."

2 "Guarantee me six things and I shall assure you of paradise. When you speak, speak the truth; keep your promise; discharge your trust; guard your chastity, and lower your gaze; and withhold your hands from highhandedness."

"Surely truth leads to virtue, and virtue leads to paradise."

Muslims discussing the Hadiths

Two "brother" Muslims

3 "Do not quarrel with your brother Muslim, nor jest with him, nor make him a promise that you cannot keep."

"Each of you is a mirror of his brother; if you see something wrong in your brother, you must tell him to get rid of it."

"Believers are like the parts of a body to one another, each part supporting the others."

"None of you can be a believer unless he loves for his brother what he loves for himself."

"A Muslim is he from whose tongue and hands other Muslims are safe."

4 "Every good action is a charity and it is a good action to meet a friend with a smiling face."

"There is a man who gives charity and he conceals it so much that his left hand does not know what his right hand spends."

"Wealth does not come from abundance of goods but from a contented heart."

5 "The best of you is he who has learned the Qur'an and then taught it.

"The seeking of knowledge is a must for every Muslim man and woman."

"The learned men are the successors of the prophets. They leave behind knowledge as inheritance. One who inherits it obtains a great fortune."

Understanding the Word of Allah

The teachings that Muslims follow have been revealed by Allah in the Qur'an or peserved in the Hadiths that record the prophet Muhammad's words and deeds. Muslims believe that the revelations from Allah in the Qur'an are unchangeable.

However, the question may be asked how reliable this revelation is, given that it is human beings who have spread the message and have written it down. In other words, what does it mean to talk about Allah's revelation as "true"?

Fundamentalist scholars are so sure of the **faith** and trust that they have in Allah that they are confident enough to say that every word of the Qur'an and the Hadiths is true. Even though the words have been written down by human beings, fundamentalists believe that they are Allah's words and they have never been changed. They are true at all times and in all situations.

Liberal scholars view the revelations of Allah as true. However, rather than being true word for word, they see them as being true in the way in which poetry is true. Poetry is full of imagery and symbol, myth and metaphor, and so is true at different times for those who write it and for those who read it.

The Muslim understanding is that there are differencesin interpretation, different ways to consider the texts "true." A Hadith illustrating this reads:

"Difference of opinion in my community is a blessing for the people."

Celebrating Festivals

In this section you will

- find out about the great Muslim festivals of Id-ul-Fitr and Id-ul-Adha;

- read about how celebrating these festivals strengthen both personal faith and community spirit;

- learn the importance of celebrating religious festivals.

Festivals in Islam

There are two great **festivals** in Islam, **Id-ul-Fitr,** which ends the fast of Ramadan, and **Id-ul-Adha,** which occurs during the month of Hajj, the time of pilgrimage to Mecca. Both are seen as occasions on which to give thanks to Allah for His blessings and kindness.

Both festivals involve worship and care for others. The whole family (**ummah**) of Islam can feel very much together, all Muslims celebrating these festivals around the world, enjoying a time with loved ones and sharing this good feeling by supporting all those who are poor or suffering in any way.

The requirements for feast days are simple:

- Cleanliness—baths are taken and clean or new clothes are worn.

- Prayer—Muslims come together in huge gatherings, to be as one. This is a powerful example of the ummah—the Muslim community.

- Thought for one's own family—presents are given, especially to children, and special meals are served.

- Thought for others—**zakah** is collected and sent off, and strangers are welcomed to share in the hospitality.

After visiting the mosque on feast days, Muslims often go home by a different route from the one they took coming, in order to create the largest possible opportunity for meeting other Muslims and spreading joy.

Id-ul-Fitr

Id-ul-Fitr is the celebration of the end of Ramadan, the month of fasting. The festival begins at the sight of the new moon that welcomes the start of the new month. Muslims celebrate by decorating their houses, giving and receiving cards and gifts, and attending special prayers at the mosque.

Zakah for Id-ul-Fitr is a special payment of a set amount, the equivalent of two meals. This is to be given to the poor on behalf of each member of the family by every Muslim who is financially able to do so.

A Muslim dressed for Id

Id-ul-Adha

Id-ul-Adha is important for two reasons. First, it marks the end of the Hajj, the pilgrimage to Mecca. Second, it recalls the faith in Allah displayed by the prophet Ibrahim when commanded to sacrifice his son, **Isma'il.**

As with the celebrations of Id-ul-Fitr, cards and gifts are given and received. However, the most important feature of the festival of Id-ul-Adha is the sacrifice of an animal to Allah. The sacrifice recalls the sacrifice of the ram that Allah provided for Ibrahim so he would not have to kill his son, Isma'il. Muslims may sacrifice sheep, goats, cows, and camels. Muslim families enjoy a big meal using the meat from their sacrifice, and share the remaining meat with the poor of the community or with friends and relatives.

"I enjoy celebrating Id because it's thanking Allah for the family and friends we have and sharing a happy time with them."

Shamira, aged 13

The Muslim festivals

Each month in the Muslim calendar follows a lunar cycle, and is 29–30 days long. Because of this, the Muslim year is a few days shorter than a Western year, and Muslim festivals, although they fall on the same day in the Muslim calendar, fall on different dates in the Western calendar.

These are the dates of the most important Muslim festivals.

1 Muharram: the Day of Hijra (the Muslim New Year, which remembers Muhammad's journey from Mecca to Medinah)

10 Muharram: Ashura (commemorates the martyrdom of Imam Husayn; mainly a Shi'ite [see page 35] festival)

12 Rabi ul-Awwal: Maulid ul-Nabi (Muhammad's birthday)

27 Rajab: Isra" wal Mir'aj (Muhammad's night journey, when he was taken to heaven)

27 Ramadan: Lailat-ul-Qadr (the Night of Power, when Muhammad began to receive the Qur'an)

1 Shawwal: Id-ul-Fitr (celebrates the end of the month of fasting)

10 Dhul Hijja: Id-ul-Adha (remembers the story of Ibrahim and Isma'il)

Celebrating in the love of Allah

Pilgrimage—Hajj 1

In this section you will

- learn the reasons for making a pilgrimage to Mecca;
- find out about the nature and importance of entering the state of **ihram;**
- read about the spiritual transformation that Hajj can have in the lives of Muslim pilgrims.

Pilgrimage to Mecca

Hajj is the fifth pillar of Islam. It is a pilgrimage to Mecca and it is to be made at least once in a lifetime by those Muslims who can afford to do so.

When Muslims pray they face the direction of Mecca. In fact they face the **Ka'bah,** the House of Allah, which Muslims believe was built originally by Adam (the first man), and later rebuilt by the prophet Ibrahim and his son, Isma'il. It was the first house ever built for the sole purpose of the worship of Allah. Muslims believe that Allah has blessed the Ka'bah. Every year Muslims who can afford to make the journey and are physically fit come here from all over the world to join fellow Muslims in worship in the House of Allah.

During Hajj the Islamic community (the **ummah**) becomes particularly evident and can be experienced in a special way by everyone who takes part. Barriers of language, territory, color, and race disappear as the bond of faith is strengthened. Everyone has the same status in the House of Allah—the status of His servant.

The Ka'bah

"It was the most amazing moment of my life. Standing before God at the foot of Mount Mercy with 2,000,000 of my fellow Muslims really did bring my faith alive for me. I have always tried hard to keep the teachings of the qur'an, but this was different. Everything that I have ever been taught, the events in the life of the Prophet that I had only heard about, was real. To bear witness with so many others is an experience that I shall never forget."

Mamood, aged 24—Hajji (pilgrim)

Muslims in ihram

Ihram

While approaching Mecca before the Hajj begins, a pilgrim must put on **ihram.** For men ihram consists of two sheets of unsewn white cloth, a very simple form of dress that they must wear in place of their normal everyday clothes. For a woman ihram does not require special clothes, but they do have to dress simply and wear a veil covering their hair.

This change is significant. It reminds pilgrims of their position in relation to Allah as humble servants of the Creator. It also reminds them that after death, they will be wrapped in white sheets, ideally the very same ones worn on the Hajj, not in expensive or fashionable clothes.

There are restrictions on pilgrims while in the state of ihram. He or she must not:

- use perfume;
- kill or harm animals, even insects;
- break or uproot plants;
- do anything dishonest or arrogant;
- carry weapons;
- cover the head (males);
- cover the face (females);
- wear shoes covering ankles;
- cut hair;
- clip nails;
- have sexual relations.

United before Allah

Hajj brings together Muslims from all around the world. It also brings together Muslims from the two main groups within Islam—Sunni Muslims and Shi'ite Muslims.

Following the death of Muhammad there were disagreements about who should lead the Muslims. Those who supported the prophet's descendants as leaders became known as the "Shiat Ali" or the Party of Ali. They are now called Shi'ites. They do not accept the first three **khalifahs** who ruled Islam following the death of Muhammad. They claimed that Ali was really the first true leader after Muhammad, followed by the prophet's grandsons Hasan and Husayn.

Sunnah is the Arabic word for "custom," "authority," or "pathway." Sunni Muslims regard themselves as the true followers of the Sunnah, or the example of the prophet Muhammad. They say that Muhammad intended elections by consensus so that the best man would succeed as leader, and not to start a family line of rulers.

Eighty-five percent of all Muslims are Sunnis. The Shi'ites make up only 15 percent of modern Muslims, although in some places like Iran, most Muslims are Shi'ites.

Pilgrimage—Hajj 2

In this section you will

- find out about the duties performed by Muslims on Hajj;

- read the story of why Mina is a place of importance to Muslims;

- learn the importance of each duty of hajj.

The duties of Hajj

Muslims performing Hajj and in a state of ihram can truly be described as one equal family before Allah. It is as one family that the essential duties or rituals of Hajj are performed.

- The **Ka'bah** is circled seven times. The Ka'bah is thought by Muslims to be the very first place used to worship Allah. Pilgrims run between the hills of **Safa** and **Marwah** where **Hajar,** wife of the prophet Ibrahim, desperately searched for water for her child.

Allah provided water in the form of the Well of Zamzam, where pilgrims still stop to drink and to fill bottles to take some of the water home.

- Pilgrims then travel out of Mecca along the plain of **Arafat.** Here around two million pilgrims camp as they perform the next duties of Hajj.

- Pilgrims stand together before Allah on Mount Arafat (The Mount of Mercy). It is an opportunity to commit oneself again to Allah and to follow His laws in all aspects of life.

- The camp then moves on to Muzdalifah, which is between Arafat and Mecca. Here pilgrims collect small stones to throw at the pillars at **Mina.**

- Mina is where the prophet Ibrahim and his family resisted the temptations of the Devil to turn away from Allah and put their trust in him. Pilgrims throw stones at three stone pillars that represent the Devil. This symbolizes a rejection of both the Devil that tempted Ibrahim and also at the "devil" inside that leads everyone into temptation.

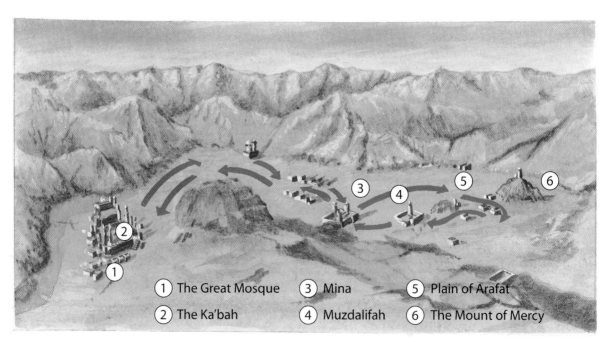

| 1 | The Great Mosque | 3 | Mina | 5 | Plain of Arafat |
| 2 | The Ka'bah | 4 | Muzdalifah | 6 | The Mount of Mercy |

The route of the Hajj

- The pilgrims then camp at Mina for two days to celebrate the Feast of Sacrifice (**Id-ul-Adha**). An animal is sacrificed in thanksgiving for the ram Allah gave Ibrahim just as Ibrahim was about to sacrifice his son, Isma'il, to Allah.

- As an outward sign of the completion of the duties of Hajj, men have their heads shaved (unfurling) and women will have about 1 inch (2.5cm) cut from their hair.

- Pilgrims then return to Mecca to circle the Ka'bah again before returning to their homes.

Male Muslims who have performed Hajj are entitled to take the name **Hajji,** and women the name **Hajjah.**

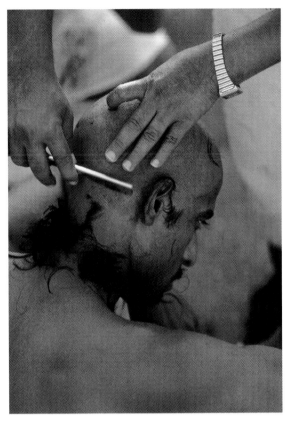

The unfurling

Id-ul-Adha

Id-ul-Adha remembers the story of Ibrahim told in the Qur'an—a story of unwavering **faith** and submission to Allah's will.

Ibrahim had made a promise to dedicate his life to the will of Allah. One night Ibrahim had a dream in which he was asked to sacrifice his only son Isma'il to Allah. He was distraught, but he spoke to his son and they agreed to do what Ibrahim had been commanded to do.

They travelled to Mina, where the sacrifice was to take place. Isma'il lay face down on the altar, ready to be sacrificed. At the last moment, however, Allah stopped Ibrahim and gave him a ram to sacrifice in place of his son.

Rules for pilgrims

Muslims who perform Hajj must first fulfill certain criteria. First of all, they must be Muslims—non-Muslims are not permitted to take part in the pilgrimage. They must be physically fit and mentally sound, so that they can cope with and fully understand the purpose of their actions. They must also have enough funds both to pay for their pilgrimage by honest means, and to support any dependents they leave behind during Hajj.

Rites of Passage

In this section you will

- discover the ways in which Muslims celebrate birth;
- read about the importance of marriage in the Islamic community;
- discover how the tradition of prearranged marriage may be changing in parts of the Islamic community.

Everyone enjoys a celebration. Finding an excuse for a party or sharing a good time with family and friends is not difficult. However, the reasons behind some celebrations are very important—the birth of a baby or the joining together of two people in marriage are important to both religious and nonreligious people alike. This is an opportunity to discover how Muslims mark these two special occasions, referred to as rites of passage, in a special way.

Birth

For Muslims the birth of a baby is a reason for great joy. Muslims believe that Allah has granted the family the blessing of a son or daughter, so He should receive their thanks and praise.

A newborn baby hearing the adhan for the first time

The new baby is welcomed into the community of Islam as soon as it is born, as the head of the family whispers the adhan (the call to prayer) into its ear. Therefore, the first word the baby hears is "Allah." In some Muslim cultures, prayers, usually led by the community's imam, are said for the baby and the family.

Marriage

Muhammad said:

"A woman should only be married to a person who is good enough for her or compatible to her."

Hadith

For Muslims the only sort of compatibility that really matters is faith. Muhammad permitted marriages between people of vastly different social status and financial backgrounds, knowing that compatibility depended more on what they were like in their hearts and in their devotion to Allah. In fact, Islamic law allows Muslim men to marry Jewish or Christian women, recognizing how much is shared by these three "religions of the book" (scriptures).

The most important ingredients in a Muslim marriage are shared values and **beliefs,** so that even if the couple come from different cultures and backgrounds, they will possess the same basic religious attitudes and practices that will help bind them closer together.

"Do not marry only for a person's looks. Their beauty might become the cause of moral decline."

"Do not marry for wealth, since this may become the cause of disobedience. Marry, rather, on the grounds of religious devotion."

Hadiths

A Muslim marriage

Islam regards marriage as the normal duty of every human being. Finding a good life partner and building a relationship together is regarded as an essential part of the faith.

The Muslim marriage service is a social ceremony rather than a religious one, so it can take place anywhere that is licensed for marriages. However, the marriage contract can also be completed before someone qualified in Islamic law.

In the Muslim world, there is often little contact between young men and women. The selection of marriage partners is often made by the parents, although the bride must approve of her future husband. For these couples love is expected to come after marriage and not before. In some Muslim families, customs are changing a little in regard to this custom, with some couples deciding for themselves their own suitability for each other.

"The best of treasures is a good wife. She is pleasing in her husband's eyes, looks for ways to please him, and takes care of his possessions while he is away. The best of you are those who treat their wives best."

Hadith

Muslim names

Seven days after the birth of a Muslim baby comes the celebration of aqiqah. This is when relatives and friends come to a feast and the baby is named.

First of all, the baby's head is shaved, and by tradition gold or silver of the same weight as the hair is given to the poor. Even if the baby has no hair, a donation of money is still given. Some Muslims also offer a sacrifice, a sheep or a goat, for a feast with friends to give thanks for the birth.

The choice of name is important. In fact, choosing the name is seen as one of the most important duties a parent can carry out. The chosen name is usually a family name or one of the names from Muhammad**'s** family.

For boys, some of the names often chosen start with "**Abd,**" which means "servant." Abd will be added to one of the 99 different names for Allah, for example, Abdullah (Servant of God), Abdul Rahman (Servant of the Merciful) and Abdul Karim (Servant of the Generous One). This shows that whatever else they may do or become in life, it the first duty of every Muslim to be a faithful servant of Allah.

Khitan

All Muslim baby boys are circumcised. This involves cutting the foreskin from the penis. Circumcision is the ancient practice of the prophets and is seen as a special sign to show that one belongs to Allah. Circumcision is not regarded as cruel. It is in fact seen by some as a healthy practice, although within the Islamic community there is some debate on the issue.

Creation

In this section you will

- find out about Islamic beliefs regarding the creation of the universe;
- read how the Islamic beliefs about creation compare with those of Jews and Christians;
- learn how Islamic food laws reflect Muslims' care and respect for the body.

Earth from space

The power of Allah

Most religious traditions have developed an account of **creation** that depicts the central involvement of God. The Koran is very clear as to the origins of all things. All things derive their being from Allah and to Allah shall all return when their time is over.

"It is Allah who has created the heavens and the earth, and all that is between them in six days. Then he rose to His throne that suits His majesty. Mankind has no God besides Allah, as protector and helper. Remember this, Allah manages and regulates everything on Earth and in Heaven and when everything has had its time, it will return to Him."

"Allah alone is the all-knower of the seen and unseen, the all-mighty, the most merciful. It was He who created all goodness and began the creation of mankind from clay. Then He made offspring—male and female. Then He made all other living things upon Earth."

Qur'an, surahs 21 and 32

At the completion of His creation, Allah declared:

"Have they not looked at the heaven above them, how we have made it and adorned it, and there are no rifts in it?

And the Earth! We have spread it out, and set thereon mountains standing firm, and have produced therein every kind of lovely growth in pairs."

Qur'an, surah 50:6–7

The creation

Muslims have a very clear understanding of how the whole universe came about: It was created by Allah. The **Qur'an** teaches that all things were summoned into existence at Allah's command in pairs so that creation may be in perfectly balanced order. This balance can be seen in the sky and the earth, the oceans and dry land, light and darkness, and male and female.

In common with the Jewish Torah and Christian Bible, the Qur'an tells of creation covering six days. However, a "day" can be understood in many ways. Some Muslims believe that "days" mean stages of creations and not time. Muslims are certain that if Allah had wished, He could have created everything in a moment.

Similarly, the Qur'an mentions the creation of beings that are not mentioned in either the Torah or Bible.

For example, Muslims believe in common with Jews and Christians that human beings were created from clay. They also believe that **angels** (servants of Allah who always do His will) were created from light, and that **jinn** (beings created with free will, living on Earth in a separate, yet parallel, world to our own) were created from fire. However, of all of Allah's creations, this planet and, in particular, the human beings that inhabit, it are the most important.

A famous story illustrates the importance of the creation of humans. After the creation of Adam, the first man, Allah brought all the angels and the jinn named Iblis before Adam and commanded them to bow down to him since he was the most wonderful thing that Allah had ever created. All the angels bowed down, but the jinn defied Allah and refused. As a punishment Allah banished Iblis from His presence. In return, Iblis (now known as Shaytan, fallen one, evil one, Satan) vowed to spend all his time and power tempting humans to go against the will of Allah and to sin.

Haram foods

Haram (prohibited) foods include:

- any products made from a pig;

- meat containing blood;

- meat from an animal which dies due to disease or other natural causes;

- any flesh-eating animal;

- any animal that has been killed either by another animal or by any means made haram by Allah;

- any animal that has been sacrificed to idols.

Food laws

Like many other religions, Islam teaches that some foods are allowed (**halal**) and some foods are forbidden (haram).

Muslims are allowed to eat all types of fruit, vegetables, and grains. The main restrictions are related to animal products. In order to be halal, an animal that is killed has to have all the blood in it drained away. Islamic law requires the animal to be killed by a sharp knife in the neck, which allows this to happen. Allah's name is repeated over the animal to show that the food is being taken with God's permission.

Meat of animals not slain in this way is regarded as haram. Even the marrow, rennet (stomach enzyme for making cheese), and gelatine of these animals are haram. Efforts are made to obtain halal meat from Muslim butchers, and Muslims have to take care that they do not eat haram food "hidden" in other products.

Environment

In this section you will

- learn about the Islamic belief that all creation is Allah's;
- read about the Islamic belief that Allah has placed humans on Earth to act as His stewards;
- read about Muslims' claim that humans do not always live up to the responsibilities Allah has given them.

Allah's gift of creation

Muslims believe that Allah has given this planet to humankind to look after and protect. The **Qur'an** teaches that human beings have been created by Allah and placed on Earth to act as stewards (**khalifah**) and take responsibility for every part of Allah's creation. They are expected not to pollute or damage the world, but to protect the fine balance that makes up Allah's creation. As a result Muslims are commanded to make careful use of resources like water, respect animals, and replace used natural resources wherever possible.

"It is He who has made you custodians, inheritors of the earth."

Qur'an, surah 6: 165

Care for all creatures

Muslims believe they can expect to be judged by Allah on their stewardship of His creation, including all creatures and all the natural resources which He has given.

Many Muslims are concerned with the well-being of the other creatures, besides human beings, that Allah has placed on the planet. It is true that some animals have been given by Allah as food but Muhammad banned any "sport" that involved making animals fight each other, which was common in his time. Therefore, modern "blood sports," such as dog-fighting, are condemned by Islam.

Islam teaches that no one should ever hunt just for amusement. Muslims believe that people should only take the life of animals for food or another useful purpose.

A tropical rain forest

Respecting all that Allah has created

"If someone kills a sparrow for sport, the sparrow will cry out on the Day of Judgment, 'O Lord! That person killed me for nothing! He did not kill me for any useful purpose!'"

Hadith

All hunting should be for food, and any animal used for hunting should be well trained and kept under control.

Experiments are sometimes carried out on animals today for a variety of reasons. Some of these are for medical, others for cosmetic, purposes. The principle of compassion and kindness toward all of Allah's creations forbids any experiment simply for the development of luxury goods. Muslims should always find out if the things they buy have been produced using **halal** (permitted by Allah) methods.

If there is no possible alternative to animal experimentation in medical situations, then Muslims might accept it. However, they would prefer to look for some other method of obtaining the desired information.

"Allah, it is He who has subjected … to you all that is in the heavens and all that is in the earth."

Qur'an, surah 45: 12–1

Human responsibility

Muslims believe that Allah has given people free will and it is as free agents that we decide how we treat the planet we live on. However, Islam teaches that this planet is a place created out of love, and therefore, it should be looked after with love.

Islam teaches that Muslims should try to live at peace with nature, and to bring about a oneness between human beings and the rest of Allah's creation.

The Assisi Declaration of 1986

In 1986 Muslims were among the representatives of all the major world religions meeting in Assisi. They met to discuss the role they intended to play in the world as people of faith. Most importantly, they explored their role in looking after the world for the use and enjoyment of future generations.

The place and timing of the meeting was no accident. Assisi was the home of a man called St. Francis. Although a Christian, he has been accepted by many people of different faiths as someone who had a particular love for nature and cared for it deeply.

1986 marked the 25th anniversary of the World Wide Fund for Nature, an organization set up to work on behalf of the earth's natural environment in the face of ever-expanding world industrialization.

All the different faiths made statements regarding "religion and nature." Muslims declared: "Allah's trustees are responsible for maintaining the unity of His creation, its flora, its fauna, its wildlife and natural environment … Unity cannot be had by setting one need against another or one end over another; it is maintained by balance and harmony."

Abuses of Allah's Creation

In this section you will

- read about the Islamic view of creation as Allah's gift to humanity;

- learn about ways in which people abuse Allah's gifts;

- read about how living in a multicultural society demands respect toward all people.

The **Qur'an** teaches that we have been placed on earth to act as stewards (**khalifah**). This means to look after Allah's creation on His behalf. Sadly, there is a good deal of evidence to suggest that we do not always do a very satisfactory job. Many people abuse Allah's creation by misusing nature and, worse still, by abusing the greatest of all of Allah's creation, themselves.

The planet

Abuse of Allah's creation goes on all around the world. One of the main concerns is the way the vast tropical rainforests are being cut down at a very fast rate. It may be that the timber being cut is required for building projects, or the land being cleared is needed to graze herds of cattle, but the rainforests have been provided in nature for a particular reason. Carbon dioxide, produced when something is burned, is turned into oxygen by trees. The more trees, the more oxygen, but fewer trees means more carbon dioxide in the atmosphere.

Ourselves

Another concern of Muslims is ways in which people abuse themselves by the use of substances and intoxicants. The use of alcohol is forbidden in Islam. This applies not only to wine,

Destroying the rain forest

Muhammad spoke out against the use of alcohol.

which existed at the time of Muhammad, but also to any other form of alcohol. The main reason for this is that alcohol can cause people to lose control over their own minds and bodies. A respectful, devotional frame of mind cannot be reached when a person is confused by intoxication.

"Approach not prayer if you are intoxicated...."

Qur'an, surah 4:43

"They ask thee concerning wine and gambling. Say:'In them is great sin, and some profit (usefulness), for men; but the sin is greater than the profit.'"

Qur'an , surah 2:219

"O you who believe! intoxicants and games of chance…are only an uncleanness, Shaytan's work; shun it therefore that you may be successful. Shaytan only desires to cause enmity and hatred to spring in your midst by means of intoxicants and games of chance, and to keep you off from the remembrance of Allah and from prayer. Will you then desist?"

Qur'an , surah 5:90-91

Islam teaches that Shaytan (Satan) uses different ways to turn people away from belief in Allah, and alcohol is just one. At the time of Muhammad, many people enjoyed drinking alcohol. The teaching of Allah in the Qur'an took human weakness into account, and the prohibition of alcohol was given in stages.

Living with respect

We as human beings are but a small part of Allah's universe. However, we are a very important part because Allah has granted us stewardship of his creation.

Many people would want to suggest that the best way to look after the country in which we live is to begin by treating all those that live in our society with respect. Only by working together can we treat our environment with respect.

The United States is a multicultural society. This means that people from a wide variety of religious, national and ethnic backgrounds live in the United States today. Two hundred years ago it may have easily been assumed that your neighbors would have been white, of European descent, and claim to be Christian. Today this is not the case. In 2002, 33 percent of the population was made up of ethnic groups other than "white" (this percentage does not even necessarily include Hispanics, who are counted under the categories of black, white, Asian, or other). This figure of 33 percent is expected to keep increasing. Living together with mutual respect is a positive way to look after Allah's creation.

"Prejudice" means prejudging someone or a group of people, usually in a bad way. "Discrimination" means acting unfairly toward someone or a group of people based on prejudged ideas.

Both prejudice and discrimination are wrong and have no place in devout people's lives.

Human Rights

In this section you will

● discover what is meant by "human rights";

● read about the importance of basic human rights for Muslims.

Human rights and responsibilities

Islam teaches that all human beings have been created by Allah. As a result Muslims believe that there are basic rights that are shared by all people and that should be observed in every society, whether the society is Islamic or not.

These human rights have been granted by Allah, and not by any ruler or government, and it is the duty of Muslims to protect them actively. Failure to do so can lead to people being oppressed and living life in misery. Muslims believe that human life is sacred, and that all human beings should be treated with respect.

The earth has many wonderful resources, and there is enough for everyone to live well. No human being should know hunger while others are able to waste what they have. Islam teaches that the needs of the suffering must be met. The hungry should be fed, the naked clothed, and the wounded or diseased given medical treatment, whether they are Muslim or not, and whether they are friends or enemies.

The ummah before Allah

Sufferers of famine

Muslims also believe that the honor and dignity of every individual is important. Therefore, ridicule is never seen as fun, especially when there is arrogance or malice behind it. Muslims believe that we may laugh with people, to share in the happiness of life, but we must never laugh at people or do anything else to cause them distress or embarrassment.

Muslims believe that no attempt should ever be made to force people to act against their own will, as long as they are not acting against the best interests of others. Muslims also believe that no human being should ever be imprisoned, unless he or she is proven guilty of some crime, in an open and unbiased court.

Muslims believe that the power of any human being is only given in trust from Allah. It is, therefore, people's duty to speak out against dictators and protect the weak from those who would oppress them. To Muslims a dictator is a ruler who attempts to assert his own will on the people rather than seek for them the will of Allah, which is always based on kindness and justice.

Protecting people's freedom

It is the duty of an Islamic state to promote right and forbid wrong (**Qur'an, surah 22: 44**).

According to the Qur'an, the state is responsible for the welfare of all its citizens—Muslims and non-Muslims alike. It should grant the basic necessities of life. All citizens of an Islamic state should enjoy freedom of belief, thought, conscience, and speech. Every citizen should be free to develop their potential and earn a living wage. All citizens should enjoy the right to speak out on issues they consider right or wrong, knowing that the Islamic state is bound by duty to implement the laws of the Qur'an.

Some Muslims are disappointed that there is not a single perfect Islamic state in the world today. There are many countries that claim to be "Islamic," but some critics, Muslims and non-Muslim alike, argue that much of the time they fall short of true Islamic ideals. Many feel that a true Islamic state should be based on the model of prophet Muhammad**'s** state in Medinah.

Some Muslims today are working to bring into being true Islamic democracy. However, organized efforts are being made in many parts of the world to bring about total change in society by setting up an Islamic system of government to fully implement the laws of the Qur'an. It is hoped that Islamic states will emerge from these efforts that will guide the problem-torn world toward justice, happiness, and peace.

Caring for Others—Zakah

In this section you will

● learn about zakah, the third pillar of Islam;

● read about ways in which zakah can make a difference in the lives of all Muslims;

● learn how Muslims regard zakah as caring for others and creating fairness in society.

A Muslim making a zakah contribution

Caring for others

All Muslims are expected to be charitable in hospitality and in caring for the wider community. For example, a baker's shop could give away what it had left on a Thursday night, so that no one nearby has to say their Friday prayers hungry. Similarly, a Muslim could send money to support a good cause or disaster fund.

The prophet Muhammad encouraged giving:

"He who eats and drinks while his brother goes hungry is not one of us."

Hadith

"Every day, two **angels** come down from Heaven; one of them says, 'O Allah! Compensate every person who gives in Your name.' The other says, 'O Allah! Destroy every miser!'"

Hadith

Zakah

In addition to such voluntary charitable giving, Muslims are expected to share their income and wealth as a matter of duty, and to contribute a certain amount each year to support the less fortunate in the community. This is regarded as a religious duty, not a choice, and is called **zakah**.

Zakah is the third pillar of Islam. The Arabic word "zakah" means "to purify or cleanse." Zakah is to be paid once a year. It should be 2.5 percent of the savings you have had for a complete year. Payment of zakah is a way to stay clear of greed and selfishness. It also encourages Muslims to be honest.

Zakah is a mandatory payment and is not seen by Muslims as a charity or a tax. Charity is optional and taxes can be used by the state for any purpose, but zakah has to be spent for purposes like helping the poor and the needy, paying salaries to its collectors, freeing captives

Helping the poor

Rates of zakah

Wealth	Minimum amount on which zakah is due	Rate
Cash in hand or bank	595 grams of silver	2.5%
Gold and silver	85 grams of gold or 595 grams of silver	2.5%
Trading goods	595 grams of silver	2.5%
Cows	30	1
Goats and sheep	40	1
Mining produce	Any	20%
Agricultural produce	Per harvest: 　Rain-watered land 　Irrigated land	 10% 5%

and debtors, and helping travelers in need. Zakah is an act of worship and obedience. Muslims pay zakah to gain Allah's favor. Zakah provides Muslims with the opportunity of sharing their wealth with those less fortunate.

Muslims see wealth as really belonging to Allah. He is seen as the real owner and people are merely the trustees of His wealth. Through the payment of zakah, the rich share their wealth with the poor, thus striving for a more equal distribution of resources.

A duty of care

Islam is a way of life. More than just a group of believers, Muslims have a duty of care for each other in the name of Allah. The way in which Muslims approach the acquisition and distribution of wealth reflects this point well.

Muslims appreciate that economics are complex, but they argue that the effort should be made to ensure a fairer distribution of wealth and resources around both the national and world economies.

The Islamic economic system

Islamic laws govern the ways in which Muslims can earn and spend their money. In addition to the duty to make zakah contributions, Muslims may not:

● earn money from the production or sale of alcoholic drinks, from gambling and lotteries;

● earn money by illegal means, such as theft, deceit, fraud, and so on;

● earn money through any transactions that involve charging interest, which Islam teaches is a means of exploitation.

Muslims see the approach of the modern "free market economy" as against the most basic of Allah's wishes for humankind—that fairness and justice should be available to all. Islam teaches that a system of zakah distributes wealth more fairly (rich to poor) than a system like a free market, which, it is said, is designed to redistribute resources from poor to rich.

Women in Islam

In this section you will

● find out what the Qur'an teaches regarding the status of women in Islam;

● read about issues relating to modern Muslim women;

● learn how Islam treats women and men as equals.

Women have a very important place in Islamic society. The importance of women as mothers and as wives was made clear by Muhammad:

"Paradise lies at the feet of your mothers."

Once, a person asked Muhammad, "Who deserves the best care from me?" The prophet replied, "Your mother, then your mother, then your mother, then your father, and then your nearest relatives."

"O people, your wives have certain rights over you and you have certain rights over them."

Muhammad also said:

"The best amongst you is the one who is best towards his wife."

Hadiths

These sayings indicate the important position granted to women in Islam. In many parts of the Islamic world, women are free to pursue any career they wish. In some places, such as Pakistan, Bangladesh, and Turkey, women have even been prime ministers, while in some parts women are not allowed to drive or travel by themselves, as in Saudi Arabia. Some people argue that in those places where Muslim women

A group of Muslim women

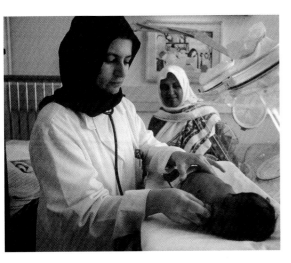

A Muslim woman at work

do not have some rights, it is a problem of the culture and not Islam, which guarantees rights to women. For instance, women have been both forced and forbidden to wear **hijab** in different parts of the Islamic world. Nothing in the **Qur'an** supports these practices. The Qur'an provided for major advances in the status of women, giving women in the region rights and protections they had not had previously, not even in Europe at the time.

A Muslim women has certain rights and responsibilities, for example, the right to develop her talents and to work. It is the duty of the Muslim mother to bring up children according to the faith of Islam and to look after the family. Islam allows a Jewish or Christian woman married to a Muslim man to keep and practice her religion, and her husband cannot interfere with this freedom.

Many Muslim thinkers believe that although women have unequal status throughout much of the Muslim world (this is also true of the non-Muslim world), if societies truly put Islamic values into effect, then Muslim women will have true equality. Some thinkers believe that a form of Islamic feminism, different from the feminism of the West, can give full rights to Muslim women and strengthen Islam.

Women and Allah

The significance of Muslim women as an important half of the human race, created and loved by Allah, is clear in this passage from the Qur'an:

"The Muslims, men and women,
the believers, men and women,
the men and women who are obedient,
the men and women who are truthful,
the men and women who are patient,
the men and women who are humble,
the men and women who give *sadaqah*
(zakah and alms to the poor),
the men and women who observe sawm,
(fasting during Ramadan),
the men and women who guard their
    chastity
and the men and women who remember
    Allah much with their hearts and
    tongues,
Allah has prepared for them forgiveness
    and a great reward (Paradise)."

One of the teachings of Islam is that men and women, although different by nature and having different social roles, are created equal as spiritual beings before Allah. All the teachings of Islam given in the Qur'an speak to both male and female Muslims.

On one occasion, the wife of Muhammad spoke to him about this. Allah provided Muhammad with a special message to explain that the term "man" in the Qur'an's revelations referred to "all human beings" and not just male human beings.

All people, male and female, are expected to follow the religion that Allah has presented to them, and they will be judged together according to their faithfulness.

Matters of Life and Death

In this section you will

- find out what "human life is sacred" means;

- learn about Islamic teachings regarding the afterlife;

- read about the Islamic teachings regarding some moral issues.

Muslims believe that all human life is a gift from Allah, and is, therefore, sacred.

"Whosoever kills a human being…it shall be like killing all humanity; and whosoever saves a life, saves the entire human race."

Qur'an, surah 5:32

"It is He, Allah, who makes laughter, and makes weeping. It is Allah who causes death and gives life. And that He Allah creates the pairs, male and female."

Qur'an, surah 53: 42–5

Muslims believe that Allah has given every life an allotted span of time. No human being knows when their life will be required by Allah and taken back. Therefore, it is the duty of all Muslims to live every day as if it was their last, in readiness for the moment when they will face Allah and answer to Him for what they have done with their lives.

"The knowledge of the final hour is with Allah; none can reveal the time but He. It shall not come upon you except suddenly."

Qur'an, surah 7:187

Islam teaches that death itself should never be feared. It is human nature to dread pain and suffering, but Muslims should do their best to bear everything with patience and fortitude. Death is the natural end of human life on earth. It cannot be avoided, and no one escapes it.

"When their time comes, neither can they delay nor can they advance it an hour."

Qur'an, surah 16:61

Muslims should not fear death, nor consider it to be the end of everything, since they believe in the promise of an afterlife. This should be a time of great joy and reward for all their efforts on Earth. In effect human life is one eternal life made up of two parts, life before death and life after death. Muslims believe that the body that Allah has creatyed will be raised by Allah, from death to the afterlife.

"Do you think that we shall not reassemble your bones? Yes, We are able to put together in perfect order the tips of fingers!"

Qur'an, surah 75:3

Islam, therefore, teaches that death is beyond human control. No person can choose the time of his or her passing—it is Allah alone who sanctions the hour of death.

A Muslim tombstone

"No person can die, except by Allah's leave, and after an appointed term."

Qur'an, surah 3: 145

After the body is washed, it is covered in cloth and buried without a coffin, except to comply with local health regulations. The body should be buried simply in the earth.

Muslims are usually buried with their face s turned toward Mecca. It is, therefore, preferable if they can have their own cemeteries or plots, so that their graves face in the right direction.

As the body is lowered, they say:

"In the name of God we commit you to the earth, according to the way of the Prophet of God."

A little earth is then thrown down with the words:

"We created you from it, and we return you into it, and from it we will raise you a second time."

Qur'an, surah 20: 55

Money is not to be spent on elaborate tombstones or memorials, but on donations for the poor. Mourning should not last for more than three days, except for widows, who may mourn for four months and ten days and should not remarry during that period.

Last words

When death is very near for a Muslim, it is important for the person to be surrounded by family and friends. The person will ask their forgiveness and Allah's forgiveness for any wrongdoing. If possible, the last words they say will be the shahadah, the declaration of **faith** in Allah.

Moral dilemmas

Muslims believe that human life is sacred. and that any taking of life, including suicide, is forbidden. The situations below are examples of moral dilemmas of the type that may face Muslims today.

1 An unmarried woman becomes pregnant and is uncertain . She is faced with a number of possibilities:

- to have the baby and raise it;
- to have the baby and put it up for adoption;
- to have an abortion (an operation to end the pregnancy).

Islam teaches that all life is a gift from Allah and, as such, should be respected. However, Islam says that the spirit that gives a person his or her unique personality does not develop until the fourth month of pregnancy. So, although an abortion would not be the ideal, it might be permissible in certain circumstances.

2 A 63-year-old grandfather is diagnosed as suffering from an incurable form of cancer. He has been told that he will die soon and will suffer a lot of pain. He asks a doctor to end his life painlessly with a lethal injection before the cancer gets worse. The request is denied.

Muslims believe that, as human life is given by Allah, it can only be taken away by Allah. No Muslim is allowed to cause a person's death even if the person is suffering. However, it is permissible not only to relieve pain through appropriate medication, but also to allow the person's natural death and not prolong it by "extraordinary measures" (artificial support such as heart-lung machines).

Jihad

In this section you will

- read about the nature of jihad in Islam;
- discover the reasons for the inclusion of jihad in the Muslim life of faith;
- learn about the strengths and weaknesses of jihad in modern society.

The nature of jihad

Jihad is an Arabic word that means "striving." Muslims use the word jihad to refer to any activity undertaken for the love of Allah. Jihad demands the use of all material and mental resources to establish the Islamic way of life. Muslims may be required to give their lives for the cause of Islam.

Muslim soldiers

"The aim of jihad is to establish peace. At first we learn to control bad desires and intentions…. This is jihad within ourselves and is the basis for the jihad that is concerned with establishing right and removing evil from lives and from society, to establish peace."

Imam Aurangzeb Khan

"'We have returned from the lesser jihad to the greater jihad. The people said, 'O messenger of God, what jihad could be greater than struggling against the unbeliever with the sword?' He replied, 'Struggling against the enemy in your own heart.'"

Hadith

Muhammad was telling his followers that the highest jihad is an inner struggle against temptation and evil within ourselves. Jihad is a basic duty for Muslims, alongside the duties of shahadah, salah, zakah, sawm, and Hajj. All these duties require jihad. They teach obedience to Allah so that Muslims may reap the reward of entering paradise when they die.

The importance of jihad

"It is most important that we try hard to practice what we say."

Imam Aurangzeb Khan

"Why do you ask of others the right conduct and you yourselves forget; have you no sense?"

Qur'an, surah 2: 44

"O you who believe! Why do you say that which you do not do? It is most hateful to Allah that you say that which you do not."

Qur'an, surah 61: 2–3

These verses clearly direct Muslims to put words into action. This can, and often does, include getting involved in charity and relief organizations like the Red Crescent (the Islamic version of the Red Cross).

While taking up arms is sometimes necessary, there are strict rules about how any war should be waged.

"Fight those who fight you, but do not be aggressive. Allah does not like aggressors."

Qur'an, surah 2: 190

A Red Crescent refugee camp

Muhammad said:

"In avenging the injuries inflicted on us, do not harm the non-belligerents in their homes; spare the women; do not injure infants at the breast, nor those who are sick. Do not destroy the houses of those who offer no resistance; do not destroy their means of subsistence."

Prayers for peace

All of the major world religions teach that at the heart of God is peace. They all have prayers for peace in a world torn apart by war.

Here are three examples:

Lord, make us instruments of your peace.
Where there is hatred, let us sow love,
Where there is injury, pardon,
Where there is doubt, faith,
Where there is despair, hope,
Where there is sadness, joy.

(Christianity)

Oh Allah, you are peace.
You are the source of peace.
You are full of blessings and sublime.

(Islam)

Cause us, our Father, to lie down in peace,
And rise again to enjoy life.
Spread over us the covering of your peace,
Guide us with your good counsel
And save us for the sake of your name.

(Judaism)

Jihad has resulted, at times, in violent struggles. For devout Muslims, wherever possible jihad is centered around changing hearts and minds by peaceful persuasion rather than by force.

Evil and Suffering

In this section you will

- read some comments about what is meant by the problem of evil;

- learn Islamic responses to the claim that blame for evil and suffering in the world should be laid before Allah;

- read a story that brings up ideas about the problem of evil.

Every day the media bring us headlines about things many would describe as "evil," or about great "suffering."

Young family dies in house fire

Man convicted of murder

Earthquake kills thousands

Famine threatens Ethiopia

Leukemia sufferer, 14, in need of emergency bone marrow transplant

The effects of an earthquake

The problem of evil and suffering

Every day people ask the question "Why?" Why, if there is an almighty God who has created all things out of love and compassion, do we suffer? It seems impossible to believe in something all-powerful and all-loving that also allows evil and suffering to exist. It would seem that either God is not all-powerful, or else not all-loving, since evil and suffering clearly exist.

"I look at the sun, moon, sky, lakes, and wonderful things like that that Allah can do. Then I look beyond these things, the wonderful things, and I see flooding, hurricanes, and droughts. I ask myself, 'How can Allah allow such things?'"

Anish, aged 13

Muslim responses

Muslims believe that Allah is indeed all-powerful and all-loving, and for that reason has granted free will to human beings. It is the murderer who freely decides to take a life.

Muslims believe that the will of Allah is beyond human understanding and, therefore, impossible to rationalize. Muslims in their prayers will often add "If Allah wills," since they believe that all things beyond our control are in Allah's hands, and that they should trust His judgment.

"Or do you think that you shall enter paradise without such trials as came to those who passed away before you?"

Qur'an, surah 2: 214

"Revile not destiny, for, behold, I am destiny."

Hadith

A personal reflection

There was once a young Muslim called Salim. One day when he was 13 years old he returned home from school and was met by his father, who told him some very sad news. Salim's father explained that his mother was suffering from cancer. It was expected that she would not live for more than 5 or 6 months.

Salim was a tense mixture of many emotions. He felt deep, deep sorrow. He felt helpless, and he even felt guilty. Most of all he felt angry—angry that Allah, a God of love and compassion, could allow such a thing to happen to his wonderful mother who, at 35, was far too young to die.

He prayed. He prayed for what seemed like hours every day telling Allah exactly how he felt. He was angry. Salim prayed that Allah would heal his mother and make her well.

His mother did not get well. She died following months of pain and distress. Salim was angry and could not understand how Allah could allow such a thing to happen.

Some time later Salim was explaining his feelings to his **imam,** who comforted him with compassionate words. The imam explained that in a very real sense Salim's mother had been made well—she had been made whole again, free from disease by the power of Allah, and she now enjoyed the beauty and tranquillity of paradise.

Although it still hurt not to have his mother alive and with him, Salim understood what the imam meant. The life that Allah has given is more than a mortal existence on earth; it is eternal life. Sadly, at some stage, all mortal bodies die, but a person's spirit lives forever.

The Existence of Allah

In this section you will

- learn about the Muslim assertion that the statement "Allah exists" is a statement of fact;
- discuss traditional arguments that have been put forward to demonstrate Allah's existence;
- consider the validity of such arguments and present alternative views.

Moved by the power of Allah

Faith and trust

To be a true Muslim, one must be able to proclaim the faith of the **shahadah**:

"Ash-hadu an la ilaha ill-Allah wa ash-hadu anna Muhammadar Rasulullah."

("I bear witness that there is no other god but Allah; and I bear witness that Muhammad is the messenger of Allah.")

For a Muslim to state "I believe" indicates an acceptance of the reality of Allah in their hearts and minds.

"We verily created man and We know what his soul whispereth to him, and We are nearer to him than his jugular vein."

Qur'an, surah 50:16

"For all who profess the shahadah, Allah is as real as the beating of their own heart. He is the creator and sustainer of all things; there is no doubt of Allah's presence in the universe, no need to prove He exists."

Imam Aurangzeb Khan

Arguments for the existence of Allah

For some people who are not monotheists, the concept and existence of Allah can be difficult to understand and accept. For this reason Muslim scholars developed an argument to prove to all people that Allah must exist.

The "Kalam argument" contends that

- all things that exist have a cause;
- it is impossible to go back forever looking for causes;

The universe—the work of Allah

- there must, therefore, have been a first cause, that was not caused itself;

- Allah is the first cause, since Allah is without cause and requires no explanation for His existence.

There are other possible arguments for Allah's existence, for example, the fact that ever since the beginning of human history people have claimed to have experienced Allah.

Similarly, the world in which we live appears well ordered, since it sits in its orbit around the sun. Maybe the conditions for life on planet Earth have been specially designed. If so, there must have been a designer. This designer must have been Allah, the only power capable of such wonders.

A last possible argument is the very fact that human beings have a sense of right and wrong, and an understanding of what is meant by right and wrong must have come from somewhere. As children we have all been taught the correct way to behave. It is argued that this teaching and guidance must have come from Allah, the ultimate lawgiver and moral guide of all.

The perfection of Allah

"Allah is perfect, therefore, He exists."

Muslims give Allah 99 different names—an attempt to express something of what they believe Allah to be like. However, these 99 names can only scratch the surface of Allah's nature. One thing is clear, however, from Allah's names: Muslims believe that Allah is perfect.

The fact that Islam teaches that Allah has all perfections can be used as a further argument that Allah must exist. Simply stated, to exist is in itself a perfection. Therefore, if Allah has all perfections, He must also possess the perfection of existence. Therefore, Allah must exist.

However, many would argue that existence is not a perfection, and here the argument fails. For Muslims, the success of this or any argument does not matter because the question of Allah's existence in simply a matter of faith and trust.

Glossary

Abd servant

Adhan call to prayer

Akhirah "the hereafter"; belief in life after death

Allah God, or the one supreme being

Angel beings created by Allah from light, who are assigned duties and always obey Allah

Belief firm conviction

Blasphemy acting or speaking disrespectfully about Allah

Du'a voluntary prayer of supplication

Faith courage to accept the challenges of belief

Hadiths sayings and traditions of Muhammad

Hajj annual pilgrimage to Mecca

Hajjah name given to a Muslim woman who has performed Hajj

Hajji name given to a Muslim man who has performed Hajj

Halal allowed by Islamic law

Haram forbidden by Islamic law

Hijab covering, usually a scarf or other head cover, worn by Muslim women

Ibadah worship, being a servant of God

Id-ul-Adha feast of sacrifice, ends the Hajj

Id-ul-Fitr feast to break the fast

Ihram state of religious "separation" or purity

Imam teacher or leader

Injil revelation given to 'Isa (Jesus)

Islam literally "submission to Allah"

Istifaa choosing or selecting, as in the calling to prophethood

Jibril (Gabriel) angel who transmitted revelations to Muhammad

Jihad striving, struggling to do the will of Allah

Jinn elemental spirit living in a aprallel world

Ka'bah "Cube," house of worship in Mecca

Kalimah Tayyibah last words spoken by a Muslim before dying

Khalifah deputy for Allah

Khitan circumcision

Khutbah sermon

Madrasah school

Mihrab archway in a mosque indicating the direction of Mecca

Minaret tower in a mosque from which the call to prayer is given

Minbar pulpit for giving Friday sermons

Mosque place for communal prayer and activities

Muslims followers of Islam

Nafl voluntary personal prayers

Pbuh "peace be upon him" (said of the prophets)

Prophets people selected by Allah to guide humans to righteousness

Qur'an holy book of Islam

Ramadan month of fasting

Risalah divine message

Salah ritual prayer five times daily

Sawm fasting from sunrise to sunset

Sharia Islamic law

Shahadah declaration of faith

Shaytan the Devil

Shirk sin of associating anything with Allah

Sohaf of Ibrahim scrolls of Abraham

Sunna practice (or way) of Muhammad's example. Considered authoritative for Muslims

Surah a chapter in the Qur'ann

Tawhid doctrine of the oneness of Allah

Tawrah revelation given to Musa (Moses)

Trust belief in the reliability or truth of something

Ummah the "family" of Islam

Wudu ritual washing before prayer

Zabur the revelation given to Dawud (David)

Zakah obligatory giving of a percentage of your savings to the poor, the needy, and other, as commanded by Allah

Places

Arafat Mount of Mercy, where Adam and Eve met after the Garden of Paradise. Muhammad's last sermon was given in a valley of Mount Arafat

Jabal-un-Nur the Mountain of Light, where Muhammad regularly prayed in isolation in a cave and where he received his first revelation from Allah

Mecca city of Ka'bah, Muhammad's birthplace

Mina place of stoning the Devil on Hajj

Safa and **Marwah** places where Hajar searched for water

People

Abu Talib uncle of Muhammad who adopted him

Adam the first created man

Dawud the prophet David, king of Israel

Fatimah daughter of Muhammad

Hajar wife of Ibrahim

Ibrahim Abraham, the "father" of Jews and Arabs, and "friend of God"

'Isa the prophet Jesus, worshiped by Christians

Isma'il the prophet Ishmael, son of Abraham

Khadijah first wife of Muhammad

Muhammad last of the prophets, to whom Allah revealed the Qur'an

Musa the prophet Moses

Suleiman the prophet Solomon, son of Dawud (David)

Index